STO

ACPL

3 1833 0160

Y0-ACG-082

DISCARDED

650.
ELLIOTT, CARTER E.
CLEAN, SOBER, AND UNEMPLOYED

Clean, Sober and Unemployed

Strategies for the Post-Rehabilitation Job-Seeker

Carter E.
Elliot

Human Services Institute
Bradenton, Florida

TAB BOOKS

Blue Ridge Summit, PA

Allen County Public Library
Ft. Wayne, Indiana

Human Services Institute publishes books on human problems, especially those affecting families and relationships: addiction, stress, alienation, violence, parenting, gender, and health. Experts in psychology, medicine, and the social sciences have gained invaluable new knowledge about prevention and treatment, but there is a need to make this information available to the public. Human Services Institute books help bridge the information gap between experts and people with problems.

FIRST EDITION
FIRST PRINTING

© 1992 by **Carter E. Elliott**.
Published by HSI and TAB Books.
TAB Books is a division of McGraw-Hill, Inc.

Printed in the United States of America. All rights reserved. The publisher takes no responsibility for the use of any of the materials or methods described in this book, nor for the products thereof.

TAB ISBN: 0-8306-2160-1

TAB Books offers software for sale. For information and a catalog, please contact TAB Software Department, Blue Ridge Summit, PA 17294-0850.

Questions regarding the content of this book should be addressed to:

Human Services Institute, Inc.
P.O. Box 14610
Bradenton, FL 34280

Acquisitions Editor: Kimberly Tabor
Development Editor: Dr. Lee Marvin Joiner
Copy Editors: Pat Hammond and Marriette Petitpas
Cover Photograph: Susan Riley, Harrisonburg, VA

Contents

Acknowledgments

My thanks to Joan E. Smith for her editorial assistance, and to Annie Elliott for proofreading and research support. We also owe a debt of gratitude to the many alcoholics, former addicts, ex-offenders and vocational virgins who were subjected to our zealous trials and errors while we searched for a way through the obstacle course.

C. E. E.

Preface

In an earlier book, *The Obstacle Course*, we gave a personal step-by-step guide toward vocational recovery for the recovering substance abuser. That book, concise and practical in its approach, has been used successfully in Veterans' Hospitals, prisons, crisis centers, and recovery groups for the past eleven years. Reviews in professional periodicals have been positive and led to the book's distribution and use in all states and parts of Canada and South America.

Clean, Sober, and Unemployed is not only a self-help book, but also a text for counselors and others in helping professions. It addresses specialized problems and obstacles you may encounter ——whether you are recovering, an abstinent alcoholic, or a vocational virgin. Vocational virgins (job seekers who have never held a permanent job) are in that category for many different reasons. Some are quietly crying for help out of their rut, and are willing to listen, sweat, and change. Some feel more secure in the familiar environment of poverty. This is *not* a book about motivating the latter.

Unfortunately, the return of alcoholics to the working world has not been recognized as a task worthy of specialized effort. Once superficial physical recovery has been attained and the mental and emotional problems of alcoholic patients are addressed, there is a tendency to consider the job done. The clients are released, and they are forced to begin a job search without specialized employment counseling.

Their files are usually closed prematurely. They still need the discipline of performing a real job search, working at it from a well-researched plan and sticking to it for eight hours a day.

Productive employment is an integral part of a successful recovery program.

For years there was a common notion that alcoholics were just like everyone else, except that they drank too much. But if recovered alcoholics, former addicts, restored mental patients, ex-offenders, and others with socially unacceptable episodes in their backgrounds were "just like anyone else," after their problems were resolved they could waltz merrily back into productive employment with only a few gray hairs to show for the gaps in their lives.

Only an alcoholic will appreciate the grim humor of the final report of an expensive government-sponsored research project concluding that alcoholics could return to social drinking provided they did it in moderation. In like manner, an alcoholic can smoothly rejoin his nonalcoholic friends in the ranks of the gainfully employed—provided he has a spotless work history, immaculate references, no police record, no history of health problems, and—well, hasn't been an alcoholic.

This is the real world. What happened really happened. You are what you are. No time for guilt or remorse. Pick up the pieces and get back to work. The world of business isn't, and never was meant to be, a rehabilitation haven. An industry will survive only if it makes money, and taking risks by hiring people with shaky backgrounds can be expensive. You will always be in competition with "Mr. Clean," and the employer will always lean toward the candidate who poses the least threat of future personnel problems.

We once watched tennis legend Bobby Riggs in an exhibition match in which he beat a respected local pro. This would have been no notable feat, except that Riggs's side of the court was cluttered with chairs and buckets of water, and he had two Great Danes on a leash! You will be walking into your job search similarly encumbered. It is our hope that this book will help you change the odds in your favor.

"Vocational virgins," those who have never held down a real job, are similarly outclassed by Mr. or Ms. Clean. In past generations, these people would simply have been classified as bums, tramps, and hobos. People who couldn't cope went to the county Poor Farm.

Now, however, many permanently unemployed people have attained a status that is acceptable in a large part of our society, and an internal air of belonging and respectable acceptance frequently exists within such a group. Once one has settled into this caste, the comfort of resignation insidiously takes over, and getting out and getting over are considered only in fantasies. In part two of this book, I have shared with you our experiences in working with vocational virgins who are not satisfied with this dismal sentence.

From an employer's point of view, the reluctance to hire a recovered alcoholic or a vocational virgin stems from the same roots. Prejudice has little to do with it; unpleasant experiences have a lot to do with it. Do not confuse the two terms.

Unless employers are very new to the game, experience has taught them an expensive lesson on odds. The odds are that if they hire men or women who have been drunks or drug users, the recruits will soon quit or have to be terminated. Likewise, the odds are that people who have never held a steady job or have only worked sporadically since leaving school will also quit or have to be terminated long before their production repays their training costs.

If employers are given this kind of derogatory information about an applicant, and have little else to go on, and if they have the choice of hiring someone else, they will *always* select someone with proven reliability. They will always select Mr. or Ms. Clean.

This book describes logical steps toward gainful employment for alcoholics who have attained sobriety and for disoriented vocational virgins. Nothing you read in the following chapters came out of a pipe dream or a theoretical thesis. We have developed these ideas from actual trial-and-error job-search situations——over and over and over——until we found a system that works——over and over and over.

Carter E. Elliott
Christiansburg, Virginia

Part One

JOB SEARCH
FOR RECOVERING ALCOHOLICS

1

COMPETING
ON AN UNEVEN FIELD

True or False? The alcoholic job seeker is an equal competitor in the job market once his addiction is under control.

What happens to jobless alcoholics after they "graduate" from rehabilitation? Are they expected to walk straight out into the real world and compete for employment with Mr. and Ms. Goody Two-Shoes and their disgustingly perfect job histories, their syrupy, glowing references, and (but of course) their absolutely spotless mental health and police records?

Our studies have shown that the percentage of active alcoholics who enter sobriety programs or treatment centers and survive to experience permanent, stable sobriety is about one in thirty. If you add the qualification of long-term, gainful employment to your definition of "stable sobriety," the odds drop considerably.

Thousands of dollars and many long hours are spent helping to heal these minds and bodies, and then they have to be turned out. They leave with their pitiful little résumé and frightening memories of failure. When the dwindling numbers return for aftercare sessions, the counselors have the heartbreaking knowledge that most of them are walking into a revolving door. The survivors will stumble back into another rehab program.

In preparing for your job search you have been urged to read the standard self-help books on job search techniques. Did you notice something similar about all of them? Did you feel a bit left out? They all seem to assume that the reader:

- graduated *magna cum laude* from Harvard Business School;
- spent two and a half years in the Navy—discharged as a Lieutenant Junior Grade with the Good Conduct Medal;
- entered a nationally known and respected firm as a management trainee;
- was continuously employed there at ever-increasing responsibilities and income until an hour and a half ago when the company moved to Taiwan;
- has one wife, three children, a home, two cars, excellent credit, paid up insurance, a healthy stocks and bonds portfolio, ten thousand dollars in a ready-access savings account, scads of glowing references, and is twenty-nine years old.

Is it any wonder most alcoholics have a little trouble identifying with that model? Your track record is different. You require specialized methods. Not only is your background different, but *you* are different. Any alcoholic who thinks he is just like anyone else, except that he can't drink, is in for a frightening and unnecessary comeuppance.

THE PERFECTIONIST WITH AN INFERIORITY COMPLEX

It is presumed that you have stopped drinking and that you are doing something positive to "stay stopped." We have found that nearly all of our successful clients are involved in continuing therapy, such as Alcoholics Anonymous. Whatever route toward permanent sobriety you are taking is a personal matter.

But there are certain common personality traits among even sober victims of this disease that have an important bearing on a quest for employment. One of these is perfectionism combined with an inferiority complex. Recognition of this common trait is vital to preparation for vocational recovery of alcoholics and victims of other substance-abuse diseases.

Please don't confuse our use of the term "inferiority complex" with the common implication of being a wimp. In the alcoholic, perfectionism and feelings of inferiority are combined into a single trait that must be faced and dealt with head on.

I recall a popular barroom "psychology test" from years back consisting of a dart board and a single dart. The participant was instructed to attempt to place the dart squarely in the center. He could throw from any distance he wished. Some would stand so close they could hardly miss; others so far back that no one could expect them to hit the bull's eye.

In either case, they were showing the alcoholic's proclivity for attempting only those tasks that can be done perfectly or for which failure can be forgiven. He would prefer spending hours or days preparing a résumé and mailing it out to exotic corporations and institutions to following a proven plan for getting live interviews——thus protecting himself from sudden, painful rejection.

Procrastination and Self-Deceit

These are two subtraits that are products of the perfectionism-inferiority combo. Rationalizing inaction is a game alcoholics play so well that they easily convince their families, counselors, and themselves that procrastination is really cautious prudence.

When an alcoholic says or thinks something about a job search that he knows is wrong, he is telling himself a lie. You know that an alcoholic can convince himself and most others (except another alcoholic and a well-prepared counselor) that black is white and that the Pope is a Muslim. A marvelous lady we like has a way of divesting herself of these little infections of self-deceit the moment they crop up. She will say aloud, "That's the biggest lie I ever told."

Polonius's advice to Laertes ends with the oft quoted, ". . . and this above all, to thine own self be true . . .." I don't care whether you ". . . canst not then be false to any man" or not; that's up to you and your conscience. But if you aren't ready to stop lying to yourself, the time and energy you spend on vocational recovery will be wasted.

SALVAGE OPERATIONS

When a business owner looks at the charred wreckage of a burned-out factory, more comes to mind than insurance and a tax write-off. The time for regret, remorse, and tears is over. How much can be salvaged for rebuilding the business? The owner must decide, as Frank Sinatra sang in his classic, to: "Pick myself up, dust myself off, and start all over again."

If you bottomed out before your funds were exhausted, then you are one of the fortunate few. You can sustain yourself and your family during a relaxed and lengthy job search (although this is an approach we do not recommend, whatever the circumstances, for reasons we will address later). But if you are like most recovering unemployed alcoholics, this decision will not be a factor. For you, it grows increasingly apparent that the only way to get a job is not to need one.

You are faced with rent, food, overdue bills, and lousy credit. You wonder if the next phone call is a job offer or another threat from the bill collectors. Will the mail bring an interview appointment or just more trouble? Will the knock on the door be opportunity, or an officer with a warrant for your arrest for nonsupport or bad checks?

Samuel Johnson must have been thinking about you when he said, "Depend upon it, Sir, when a man knows he is to be hanged in a fortnight, it concentrates his mind wonderfully."

When you were actively into your addiction, you had troubles. The troubles were real, and you knew the troubles would become tragic as your addiction progressed. But now the addiction has been arrested and we are working on the assumption that you are ready for the next step in your sobriety—vocational recovery.

There are undoubtedly some troubles that will persist well into sobriety. If you came across the line clicking your heels together and singing, "I'm in NA, and AA, and everything is okay!" you're in for a jolt. Sobriety doesn't remove DUIs, pay long overdue support, excuse scheduled court appearances, or erase memories. But most of your troubles have been reduced to problems, and problems have solutions. Some are easy and obvious; others are hard and hidden. Many are obvious and painful.

SOME IMMEDIATE DECISIONS

Several decisions must be made immediately, and if you still have any shreds of family support, the decisions should be made in consultation with them. By this time the secret is out—not that you drank or used drugs, but that you've stopped. The time has come to bite the bullet, swallow pride, and practice some practical humility. You may have to move in with family or in-laws. You may have to apply for food stamps. You *must* make peace with your creditors. These are hard pills for the alcoholic to swallow. It flies in the face of the proud, self-confident fantasy that you nurtured for so many years.

Food Stamps

Food stamps were designed as an emergency measure to keep body and soul together during rough times—and these sure are rough times. If it's any solace, union members staying off work to honor another union's picket lines used to qualify for food stamps. They long ago rationalized their pride and were filling out the forms before the paint was dry on the picket signs.

Credit

Unless you're at a celebrity's "Asylum for Affluent Abusers," you will either lie or laugh when anyone brings up the subject of credit ratings. In recent years con artists have advertised that they can "fix" a credit rating for a fee. There are several ways they tried to do this.

One early method was to have their customer apply for credit, say at a department store, and then flood the credit bureau with requests for credit information on the same individual. Their scam was to try to jam the pipeline so that reports would be issued showing either "no derogatory information" or "no record." This doesn't work anymore, and neither do other cute methods of tricking the credit system. Credit bureaus are sophisticated institutions that have their checks and safeguards down to a near-exact science.

You also should remove from any consideration the pushy TV ads that claim they can, for a fee, get you a "gold card" even though you have no credit. The "gold card" you receive will not be a Visa, Mastercard, or American Express gold card, but a card entitling you to make charged purchases from a catalog of overpriced junk. To cover themselves for alluding to Visa or Mastercard in the ads, they also will send along a credit card application, which will be handled (and probably turned down, if your credit is bad) through normal channels.

Know Your Credit Rating. There are several facts that you should know and make use of regarding credit. Credit reporting has a normal statute of limitations of seven years. An exception is bankruptcy, in which case they will keep track of your credit for a fourteen-year period after default. Credit information cannot, by law, be kept from the subject. You can, *and must*, request a credit report on yourself before you start your return to the real world of work. There is usually a fee for this; possibly ten dollars. If you have been turned down for credit in the past month, most states require that you be given a copy of your credit report free for the asking. You must check on the laws and practice of divulgence in your state. This you'll accomplish with a simple phone call to the local credit bureau.

Many employers include a credit check as a routine part of their preemployment investigation, and you *must* know everything the employer knows, or can find out, no matter how painful it might be. This type of overt action goes against the grain of the recovering substance abuser. Remember this maxim now, and throughout your job search: What you don't know *can* hurt you! This is not an optional step. Once you have received a copy of your credit report (it will be the same report that goes out to the subscribing public), you will have an opportunity to go over it and plan damage control.

Correcting Wrong Information. There is a possibility that misleading or incorrect information is in the report. This can, and must, be resolved with the credit bureau. You will be able to incorporate your explanation or rebuttal in the credit bureau's file on you if they do not agree to expunge controversial entries. Please obtain a copy of the pamphlet on "Solving Credit Problems" from the Federal Trade Commission, Washington, DC 20580. It's free, of course.

How to Start Damage Control. All creditors must be contacted, in writing (keep copies of the letters!). They should be informed of your temporary financial setback, and assured of your intention to honor your debts in full as soon as possible. A "good faith" payment should be enclosed, if possible.

There used to be a myth circulating among alcoholic curbstone lawyers that you could send a creditor a dollar a month forever and that would keep them off your back, since you were showing good faith. It doesn't work.

But here is something that *does* work. Almost all population centers have a Consumer Credit Counseling Service. In nearly all cities I've checked, it is known by that name, or by its initials— CCCS. These groups usually consist of retired bank officers who devote several hours each day to counseling folks who are over their heads in debt. Since these institutions are nonprofit and volunteer-staffed, their budgets probably do not permit listing in the yellow pages, so check it out in the white pages first.

If this service is available in your locality, it can be located by calling several banks or credit agencies. We say several, because the first two or three might not have the information, and it may be known by a slightly different name in your town.

They operate just as you would individually. However, they have the prestige and know-how to get your message to the right person. They will evaluate your bills, discuss job search efforts, estimate when payments might begin, then write letters to all of your creditors. They will explain your temporary problem; that you voluntarily came to them for assistance in salvaging your good name and credit rating; and that they are convinced of your intention to pay your debts in full once "out of the woods."

Two things should be noted before considering such service. First, it is always free. Absolutely and totally free. If a fee is mentioned, you have the wrong number. Secondly, once you are working, you will pay consolidated installments to the service and they will apportion it out to your creditors. Until you are on your feet, a "voluntary hold" will be placed on your ability to obtain new credit. Once this is removed, credit rating will be restored, usually to a higher line than you have had approved for many years.

THE APPEARANCE ADVANTAGE

The Appearance Advantage is another important matter that may have to be discussed in family council. You may have only five to thirty minutes to make an interview impression that could turn your life around. Male or female, you should have at least one good business suit. Present yourself to a *real* friend, or to your counselor, in your best "dress up" clothes and shoes. Together, take a hard, critical look at yourself in the bright sunshine. It probably has been a long time since that dress or suit was new and it may have seen some rough handling and waistline ins and outs.

The stickiest obstacle now is that you and your family may have gotten so familiar with your daily attire that it has become acceptable. It is like the clutter that develops in a house or office. Yesterday's paper, a child's toy, a shoe, or a stack of "to-be-filed"s in the in-box become invisible to the person who put them there days or weeks ago and who gingerly steps over them or shoves them aside.

But to an outsider, this clutter might as well be outlined in neon lights. These things concentrate the guest's attention totally, and you may as well forget making a good impression. The memory of a city dump trying to pass itself off as a home will linger long after your best efforts have faded away.

So it is with worn, dirty shoes, a frayed collar, and an ill-fitting suit. If you are not applying for a "white collar" job, it is appropriate to wear more casual clothes to an interview, but they must be clean, conservative, and in good repair. A three-hundred-dollar suit isn't necessary; discount stores can provide perfectly acceptable interview clothes at a reasonable price.

You may well have worn out your welcome when it comes to borrowing money from family or friends. However, now that your new direction is beginning to be noticed, you may be ready to practice some practical humility. Try asking a friend or relative if you can purchase some interview clothes on their charge card——to be repaid as soon as work is obtained. This will bring about a much more positive response than a request for money.

What Goes Around, Comes Around

Job counselors in the 1960s and 1970s were forever frustrated by the appearance of clients who were starting a job search. Freaked-out hair and beards, coupled with dirty jeans, ragged sandals, far-out unisex jewelry, and hip talk were all the rage. Many counselors themselves tried to dress and talk the part so as to communicate better and identify with their Age of Aquarius clients. The sad fact was that this dress and manners code was popular mainly with rock bands, the campus crowd, and the unemployed.

I participated in many studies with graduate students who were majoring in counseling——a relatively new discipline in the early 1970s. They would be asked if they could be swayed——as an employer——by beards, wild hairdos, hippie dress, and other popular fads, provided the candidate possessed all the other qualifications for a job opening. Invariably they would respond that they would judge the individual only on his or her ability to do the job. All other factors were irrelevant and would be ignored.

Later in the term, these same students monitored mock interview situations in which people who were unknown to them portrayed job applicants at an interview. Unbeknownst to the graduate students, the backgrounds, abilities, and experience of all applicants were essentially the same——only specific schools, home towns, job titles, and company names were varied. *Without exception* the same students who had said appearance was irrelevant selected as best-qualified those applicants who were either clean shaven or had exceptionally well-groomed mustaches or beards, had moderate haircuts, and wore somewhat conservative clothes. The irony was that the purpose of these demonstrations was to expose hidden prejudices lingering within the counselors-in-training. The purpose *should* have been to jar them into the real world!

The Age of Aquarius is now middle-aged, and so are the flower children and rebels of that era. Unfortunately, due to drug abuse, alcoholism, or just marijuana-suppressed ambition, many are also still chronically unemployed and regularly find their way to counseling tables along with the new wave of young faces that think *they* invented hip.

A woman sporting clown rouge, a spiked maroon mohawk, and a Punky Brewster wardrobe, and a man with a wild beard, sandals, earring, and wearing a tanktop to show off his tattoos may be announcing their individualism, but they are also proving that they are not in the job market. I know that many men wear earrings these days, but most of them are students, casual laborers, in the entertainment industry, or unemployed. Others confine their ear decorations to off-duty hours.

All things being equal, an overwhelming majority of employment interviewers will pass over the unconventional in favor of the "normal." Unfortunately, individualism in appearance is universally interpreted by employers as, "I don't take orders, or even suggestions. I'll come to work when I please, leave when I please, and do what I please while I'm here. I'll stir up trouble if it suits my immediate passion, and since I'm not burdened with all those archaic codes of dress, speech, manners, and morals, I'll steal anything that ain't nailed down."

Most importantly, the interviewer won't remember anything about the applicant *except* his or her appearance. Not the four-point college transcript; not the excellent test scores. Nothing. "Sorry, we're not hiring bizarre today."

THE IMPORTANCE OF 'CHUTZPAH'

A final word concerning an important quality you should try to adopt. Alcoholism has been called the Equal Opportunity Disease, as it crosses all boundaries of race, ethnicity, cultural, and economic status. We do know, however, that there is a much higher predisposition for alcoholism among certain groups than others. In the United States, the incidence of alcoholism is quite high among Native Americans and people of Irish and Polish extraction. We have heard alcoholism called the Irish Virus and the Polish Plague. While we have known many Jewish alcoholics, and they have suffered as pitifully with the disease as their Gentile covictims, alcoholism is less prevalent among Jewish-Americans.

The reasons for this phenomenon have been the subject of many debates among students of alcoholism—intriguing, but irrelevant to our purpose here. However, we do find it interesting that people raised in the Jewish tradition rarely get hung up on the perfectionist/inferiority complex cycle that overwhelms many alcoholics running the job search obstacle course. I've wondered if a touch of *chutzpah* helped get them over the hump. The Yiddish word *chutzpah* describes the extreme drive and persistence that a recovering alcoholic or addict must develop to overcome this symptom of the disease.

2

EMPLOYMENT SERVICES: GOVERNMENT AND PRIVATE

Unemployment Insurance is one of the first matters of business you must address. You've heard about the father who put off having a "birds and bees" dialogue with his son until the boy was a teenager. When he finally announced his intention, the son replied, "Sure, Pop, what do you want to know?"

UNEMPLOYMENT INSURANCE

I sometimes feel like that father when discussing Unemployment Insurance (UI) with recovering substance abusers. You may know the ropes, and you may not. And, you may possess a great quantity of misinformation. Unfortunately, alcoholics with the most experience in the unemployment lines are frequently the same ones for whom the UI dole has been an enabler—interfering with and postponing permanent recovery.

First, let's briefly discuss the mechanics of UI. Do not confuse the Unemployment Office with the Employment Office, now officially called Job Service. Their names are often used interchangeably, but their functions are quite different. The UI office is where you register for the biweekly unemployment check, provided you have worked a minimum length of time for an employer or combination of employers over the past year. These employers must have contributed to the state UI benefits fund before an applicant can qualify for unemployment.

Who Contributes to Unemployment?

Most nonprofit organizations are not contributors to the unemployment fund. Illegal or marginally legal occupations will usually not qualify, unless the criminal employer has had the brass to register his enterprise with the state and contribute to the UI fund for his employees.

You may encounter another very important disqualifier if you have engaged in a series of subsistence jobs. You may find that you have been paid "under the table," with or without your knowledge. An employer who does not want the bother or expense of figuring out payroll deductions for federal, state, and local income tax, medical insurance, social security, and so on, may elect to hire help through agencies who specialize in providing temporary help, such as *Manpower, Inc.* or *Kelly Temporary Services*. This is perfectly legal and in many instances represents sound business judgment, since the temporary-help agency acts as a contractor and takes care of the legalities of withholding taxes and UI benefit contributions. However, an unscrupulous employer carries this idea a bit further.

For example: Sid Shaky of Fly-by-nite Industries refers to certain categories of his employees as "casual" or "contract" laborers. He pays them daily or weekly in cash. He does not keep a record of their earnings or, often, even their full names. He does not deduct for taxes or social security, contributes nothing to state UI funds, and carries no liability insurance. Often, this is a conspiracy freely entered into with the employee. Sid says, "I'd like to hire you, but I can't afford to put you on unless it's 'under the table.'" Or, "I can pay you $150 a week as a regular employee or $200 'under the table'; which will it be?"

You may have thought you were getting a good deal until: (1) you get injured and find you do not qualify for Workers Compensation; (2) you try to retire or collect Disability Income Benefits from social security and find the Social Security Administration has no record of your employment by Fly-by-nite; or, (3) things get a bit warm for Sid in that town, and one night he packs up his office and skips.

Now you report for work and find an empty building. You resign yourself to another stint of "standin' in line and signin' up." But, wait! The UI claims examiner tells you they have no record of Sid or Fly-by-nite Industries, since he did not register in that state and has made no contributions to the UI benefits fund. You are totally out of luck, and there is no appeal.

If You Quit or Were Fired

Another reason for disqualification for benefits could result from having been fired for misconduct, or quitting without very good reasons. Acceptable good reasons for quitting are rare. Simply having rotten working conditions and low wages usually won't be enough. Employers don't contribute to the state UI fund on a flat *per capita* basis. Their percentage of wages paid into the fund is affected by their layoff experience.

A druggist employing the same people continuously, year after year, will have a lower contribution rate than a dressmaker who lays off all sewing machine operators each time he retools for a style change, or sales dip a bit. Therefore, most employers will vigorously challenge any application for unemployment by anyone whom they have fired or who has quit. If the fired employee prevails and is allowed to collect UI, it affects the employer's layoff record and his contribution rate may go up.

Let's now presume you lost your job while bottoming out with substance abuse. You have stopped drinking and using and are now physically and mentally ready to proceed with a job search as part of your next step in recovery. However, you find yourself stuck in the doorway because of the typical addict conflicts of perfectionist/inferiority complex. You are terrified to attempt anything that you can't do perfectly or in which success is not guaranteed. The mere possibility of failure or rejection is ample reason to scrub the mission.

Did you work only a short time for your last employer? Usually past employment periods can be pooled to make up the required time. Were you fired? File for unemployment insurance anyway. In many states, being fired for misconduct merely entails being suspended for six to eight weeks, after which time you could reapply and collect. You may very well be needing funds; if you don't apply now, you won't have it later.

Did you quit? It is possible that you can go ahead and apply for UI, be disqualified as a matter of course, then requalify by working at a temporary job for four weeks. When you are laid off, you may become eligible for the full amount of benefits as if you had not quit your first job.

These are only examples of avenues to investigate, as state regulations vary. The purpose of unemployment insurance is to help keep body and soul together during the job search. As a recovering alcoholic, you need all the help you can get.

The important thing for you to remember is not to lie to yourself about why you don't want to take a crack at applying for unemployment. The honest answer usually is, "Because I'm terrified that they may turn me down. This is the type of situation I always handled with the help of alcohol." You can't buy *chutzpah* in a bottle anymore. You'll have to grow your own.

PRIVATE EMPLOYMENT AGENCIES

Private Employment Agencies are purely and simply profit-making organizations. Their money comes from either the applicant or the employer, or both. This is an exceedingly competitive field, and they will not spend ten minutes with you unless they feel you: (1) will eventually come up with a sizable "consultation fee" or (2) are a salable commodity with highly marketable talents or experience.

For instance, if you are a tool-and-die maker or an accountant, you could be treated in one of two fashions. You may be asked to sign a contract in which you agree to pay the agency a percentage of your salary once you are hired. This can be a whopping amount, prorated over the first six months or year of employment.

The other arrangement is the "no-fee" deal in which the employer pays the agency a commission for finding you. Don't be fooled by the hundreds of advertisements run by agencies that say something like "Management Trainee - $18,000 to $24,000 - No Fee." These are rarely honest openings. When pinned into a corner, agencies will refer to these come-ons as "composite ads; representative of placement selections available to us." Their purpose is to bring in hundreds of queries in hopes that some of them will fit category one or category two, and a quick buck can be made.

Many private employment agencies used to try to disguise their ads to look as if they were placed directly by legitimate companies that were looking for personnel. However, you will find that most states now require newspapers to print the word "AGENCY" in small letters at the top of such ads. You also may find that the so-called "no-fee" referral will be made only after a nominal "registration" fee is paid. You would then be referred to a job you could have found in the classified section or at the state job service.

There are obvious exceptions. If your background warrants a premium for your referral, then list with a reputable private agency——but only on a bona fide "no-fee" basis. Indeed, some companies prefer to hire their specialized employees through private agencies as it saves them time by prescreening obviously unacceptable applicants. They also can give the private agency more detailed, confidential instructions as to their preferences, thus sidestepping equal employment guidelines. (Wanted: Computer Programmer - Miss America Type).

If you are considering a private agency, it is best to check first with your local Chamber of Commerce or Better Business Bureau. You also should be familiar with the laws governing private employment agencies. For this information call your state government information number to locate the regulatory board covering private agency activities. You may find that there is no such body in your state. This merely increases your responsibility to check any private agency out thoroughly *before* you get committed and contracts are signed. After that point you may find yourself in the position of trying to unscramble an egg.

Often my staff and I have tried to pick up the pieces after a corrupt agency had worked over a trusting and unsuspecting applicant. In a typical situation, a young woman was convinced to sign a contract in which she agreed to turn over twenty-five percent of her first year's salary to the agency if hired in any job to which she was referred. After the commitment was made, she was handed a mimeographed sheet listing hundreds of companies known to have large hiring turnover. She was contractually obligated to pay the agency a quarter of her small salary, should she happen to score, although she was forced to do all the legwork herself.

Some of these unsavory outfits even sent collection agencies after applicants, although they had lasted only a week or two on the job. They cited fine print in the contract stipulating liability to pay for a minimum of six months despite termination of employment. Get full names of all individuals you speak with and carry home copies of applications and contracts if possible. If a private agency pushes you to sign a document immediately on your first visit, back away.

The specialized techniques for coping with résumés, applications, and interviews covered in later chapters should be studied and applied when dealing with a private agency, as well as directly with an employer.

There is an old courtroom joke about the shyster lawyer who let slip that his client was "innocent until proven broke." We've also heard that most doctors do not like to treat alcoholics because they lie about symptoms and alcohol consumption, won't take medical advice, and won't pay their bills. Without proper preparation, you will receive the same cold reaction from a legitimate "no-fee" agency. Long ago, they found that trying to work with drunks was a waste of time and money, and they didn't stay in business by repeating mistakes.

YOUR FRIENDLY STATE EMPLOYMENT OFFICE (JOB SERVICE)

WAKE UP! If you sleep through this section you'll do so at your peril. You *must* squeeze every ounce of opportunity out of every free service available. Sometimes this will entail an attitude adjustment regarding institutions you have previously rejected as useless, and a reexamination of the expensive alternatives.

How often have I heard, "I've tried the Job Service, and they never had anything—they couldn't get me a job." Wouldn't it have been great if you had been that critical of taverns and liquor stores in the first years of drinking? Let's discuss for a moment what state employment services are and are not; what they can do and what they can't do. But more importantly, how you can use them to your best advantage. And always remember—the price is right!

The people at Job Service, the proper name for the state employment service, are not public servants; they are state employees. They get many holidays, annual leave, and sick leave, but they take home less than most factory workers. Most of them have at least a college degree, and this is *not* their chosen career.

Reality, in the Job Service, takes several forms. First, realize that many people who fill out applications and wait in line for interviews *do not really want jobs*. This comes as a shock to new, bright, eager interviewers. It is also a truism that is ideologically inconvenient for social workers to discuss, except privately within their own exclusive circles, and then in low voices.

Applicants for "employment" include many people who are on temporary lay-off from their regular jobs and seasonal workers who are forced to register at the Employment Office to collect from the *Unemployment* Office. Others go through a ritual to show a wife, mother, or probation officer an updated ID card. Recently separated servicemen can collect unemployment, although many have plans to go on to school or just sit around and "get it all together." They, too, must register for "work" to fulfill the requirements for collecting.

In the larger cities, interviewers who refer applicants to jobs learn to live with the fact that half these referrals will leave the office and go straight to a bar, or just go home, never bothering to go to the job site. Their application cards are routinely stamped "DNR" for "did not report," and the fire of dedication burns a little dimmer in the soul of the once-naive interviewer. This is the point where many of those new, bright, eager interviewers start becoming stodgy civil service paper-pushing clock-watchers.

With all these obstacles, the Job Service still houses the largest and most efficiently arranged collection of current job information in your area. This is an absolute fact—regardless of statements of salespeople for private employment services, and regardless of occasional disparaging comments from detractors (including discouraged Job Service workers themselves). This valuable information will rarely be spoon-fed to you, so be prepared to dig it out.

Counseling Services

One step removed from the interviewer/placement area is the counseling activity. Counselors have passed a more specialized civil service test and usually are required to have college credits in psychology and social science. Interviewers refer applicants to counseling when they recognize obstacles to employment that require special time and attention. These folks are specialists in the field of *vocational* counseling, and will in no way threaten or interfere with any other counseling relationship related to your recovery.

You may wish to give the Job Service counselor the name and telephone number of your rehab aftercare counselor, if you have one. When I was in Job Service management, my counselors maintained a close personal relationship with rehabilitation specialists throughout their district—a very mutually rewarding alliance. Counselors are as varied in training, talent, and personality as are bartenders (Oh, you've already noticed that!) so please be patient, do not expect miracles, and help them help you.

When you go to the Job Service and have your initial meeting with the interviewer, specifically ask for an appointment with a counselor. Depending on the case load, the appointment might take place that very morning, or in three weeks. The counseling interview will require some patience on your part. This will be especially true if you are one of the tired retreads who have been around the track a few times.

Rarely will you find a counselor who is qualified in the field of alcoholism, although they will be very interested in it, so avoid a long, academic discussion about your disease. Remember why you are there: to get every bit of free help you can.

Aptitude Testing. The General Aptitude Test Battery (GATB) will be available in the counseling section. If it isn't voluntarily offered, request it. As you start the vocational state of your recovery, it is time for a fresh, clean inventory of your talent assets. The GATB consists of a series of written and manual tests that measure specific capacities and abilities required of an individual to learn a task or job duty.

The test will usually be taken with up to ten other people and probably will require half a day. Several days later, the counselor will give you the test interpretation, based on scores in these categories:

1. *General Learning Ability* - the ability to "catch on" or understand instructions and underlying principles; ability to reason and make judgments; closely related to doing well in school.
2. *Verbal* - the ability to understand meanings of words and ideas associated with them, and to use them effectively; language comprehension, to understand relationships between words, and to understand meanings of whole sentences and paragraphs; to present information and ideas clearly.
3. *Numerical* - ability to do arithmetic operations quickly and accurately.
4. *Spatial* - ability to comprehend forms in space and understand relationships of plane and solid objects; may be used in such tasks as blueprint reading and in solving geometry problems. This is frequently described as the ability to see objects of two or three dimensions in your mind.

5. *Form Perception* - ability to recognize details in objects or pictures; to make visual comparisons and see slight differences in shapes and shadings of figures and widths and lengths of lines.
6. *Clerical Perception* - ability to notice detail in observing differences in copy, proofreading words and numbers, and avoiding errors in arithmetic.
7. *Motor Coordination* - ability to coordinate eyes and hands or fingers rapidly and accurately in making precise movements with speed; ability to make a movement response accurately and quickly. A juggler would have good motor coordination.
8. *Finger Dexterity* - ability to move the fingers and manipulate small objects with the fingers rapidly or accurately. A card shark would score high here.
9. *Manual Dexterity* - ability to move the hands easily and skillfully; to work with the hands in placing and turning motions.

As your job search progresses, you undoubtedly will be asked to take employment tests. The more of these you take, the better you will do. They are usually time tests, as is the GATB, and getting rattled will drop your score sharply. Taking the GATB under relatively nonthreatening conditions is good preparation for later pressures. Most alcoholics are perfectionists, and will get a bit more anxious than others in the room about doing well on this test. It is good conditioning for the forthcoming "real thing."

Interpreting the Tests. When the time comes for the Job Service counselor to provide the test interpretation, remember that, like bartenders, counselors range from highly skillful to inept. You do not have the task of becoming a counselor critic, but to mine the gold of free information vital to your job search. The GATB is no superscientific computerized short-cut method for job placement. It is just another tool—additional input into the decision-making mechanism.

The person who processes the tests will use a computer program to convert the scores into patterns, and these patterns represent occupational groups. Over the years, this group of tests, properly interpreted, has proven to be an accurate measure of ability to pursue an occupation successfully. The term "success" here merely means that the odds are you could hack it for three years. The GATB doesn't know if you are male of female, or if you live in a project in the Bronx or on the plains of Texas. So don't be surprised if apparently inappropriate occupations such as "cowhand" or "sewing machine operator" crop up.

This test will not show what you *should* be doing, or what you would *like* to do; it only suggests what you *could* do with average effort. The GATB does not measure motivation, which can override many obstacles. Pay attention to the Job Service counselor's interpretation of the GATB, then ask enough questions to get the whole picture. Thank the counselor for his or her time and show your appreciation for this professional service. Then, file this information away to be used with other things you are learning about the new person you are becoming in your recovery.

We have spent this amount of time on the GATB because many alcoholics find it necessary or advisable to explore new areas of employment after they get sober. You may have talents and abilities hidden away that you would not have otherwise considered. This may be because you have not been exposed to them, or because they would have been impossible to pursue during your active addiction and you subconsciously repressed any serious consideration.

Know When to Quit. Remember that Job Service counselors are trained to assist job seekers with conscious or unconscious, real or imagined obstacles to permanent employment. Rarely are they experienced in successful specialized counseling of recovering substance abusers. You already know what the obstacles are, so don't prolong your association with the counselor past the point of productivity.

Sometimes counselors will continue their relationship with a client indefinitely, helping with the job search until success is attained. For some this becomes a "Magnificent Obsession," and they devote many months, even years, to working with cases that are not and may never be ready for the giant step of vocational recovery. Obviously, the rest of their job-ready clientele suffer when they pursue this unrealistic quest.

The usual procedure, however, is for the Job Service counselor to return the job seeker to the active file or *mainstream* with the counseling notes attached to the application card to help the interviewer in further placement efforts.

Remember our earlier statement about Job Service. It bears repeating. Whatever your experiences, and regardless of prevalent opinion, the Job Service remains the best-organized resource available to you. They will have the largest selection of job openings available to you from any source——including newspapers and private agencies——and all of this is free.

The Job Service Mainstream

There are many reasons why the selection of available openings at the Job Service is diverse and voluminous. The first is that this service is also free to the employers. The second is that smart employers, who bother to learn how to use the Job Service effectively, realize that they save money and personnel time by letting this state agency select and prescreen applicants before referral.

A third reason that is little known but very important to you is that *all employers holding contracts of $10,000 or more with the Federal Government must list all of their openings under $25,000 salary* with the State Job Service. There are only two exceptions to this rule: Jobs filled through contracts with union hiring halls and those filled through internal promotions. All other openings must be listed. They also must be legitimate openings, not just a paper exercise to cover someone they just hired at the gate, or through referral from the boss's golf partner. They also must accept referrals from the Job Service on these openings. Any employer who holds a federal contract and does not abide by this mandatory listing regulation is violating federal law!

If the interviewer doesn't find a suitable opening for a referral the first day, you must simply go back the next day. You must help the interviewer help you. If you are classified as a material handler, because that was the only job you could hold down for the past few years, the interviewer won't automatically look for accounting or sales positions unless asked to do so.

In larger cities, the Job Service is broken down into Service, Industrial, and Professional/Commercial offices. There is naturally some overlap between these divisions, and if you are looking for work in both industrial and commercial areas, it may be wise to register at both offices. Technically, the interviewer at the Industrial Office can do a job search for an engineer and the Professional Office has listings for mechanics, but their expertise is usually in their assigned categories.

You must time your visits to the Job Service for the maximum advantage. If you are looking for a temporary job to tide you over and build up your working capital——one that requires little experience but pays well enough——you must get there before they unlock the door. These jobs are highly perishable and will "go up in smoke" in the first hour of the day. On the other hand, if the job you are seeking is more specialized, you may decide to check with them in mid-afternoon, when the office is not crowded and the interviewer can afford more time. This way you can get an appointment to see an employer and be at his desk at opening of business the following day.

Any opening you spot in the newspaper that looks interesting should be shown to the Job Service interviewer. Usually he or she will have some knowledge of the company and will be able to fill you in on interview techniques and pitfalls peculiar to that facility. The interviewer will be particularly helpful in checking out *blind ads*——those bearing no company name, only a phone number or address.

These interviewers make hundreds of calls to employers each day and many have developed a style for getting an appointment for their clients that is twenty-four-carat gold chutzpah. Listen and learn. Each newspaper ad that the interviewer checks out will save a phone call, a bus ride, and, most importantly——time.

3

CHANGING
THE THINGS YOU CAN

Throughout the 1990s, employers will hire the person with computer knowledge over the computer illiterate for almost any position, whether computer use is part of the basic job or not. For the recovering alcoholic seeking to reenter the workforce, now is the time to consider computer training. I don't care how qualified you were before you dropped out of sight, you are now entering a "brave, new world." Being able to use computers may give you the edge you need when competing with Mr. Clean for a job.

COMPUTER TRAINING

Eons ago, when I was in high school, the boys put typing and other commercial courses on a par with home economics and girls' gym. *Real* men took metal shop and played football. Then World War II came along, and we learned that guys who could type had clean skivvies every day and slept under a roof, while those *real men* walked an awful lot, frequently slept in wet ditches, and got shot at.

There was a time, not very long ago, when office computers were only thought of as fancy electric typewriters. The "girls" were sent to word processor training and *real men* prided themselves in their lack of comprehension of the mystique of the computer. They would joke about it, but their ignorance bothered them no more than did their non-mastery of a sewing machine. Many of those *real men* played this macho game too long and were either put out to early pasture or found themselves working *for* those real women they had demeaned.

Today, in almost every line of work, knowing how to operate a computer is as basic as driving a car or using a telephone. Warehouse supervisors keep time and attendance and production schedules on a computer. All offices are moving away from typewriters to electronic word processing. The federal government doesn't buy typewriters anymore.

There were some stubborn holdouts in fields such as sales and law enforcement who insisted that their field people weren't hired to be "typists" and required them to dictate reports for others to transcribe. The wise futurists handled this little obstacle by a shift in job description. These folks wouldn't be "typing" reports; they would be "composing" reports—*on a computer.*

A question on computer literacy is now starting to appear on *all* new job application forms and employment interview checklists. Having the ability to just say "yes" to the question of computer competency is so easy to accomplish that vocational counselors who neglect it should be considered guilty of malpractice.

You can enroll in adult education classes at the local high school, YMCA, YWCA, a local community college, and many other locations. There is usually a nominal fee charged. At this writing a basic computer familiarization course can be taken for between ten and twenty-five dollars. If it sounds like a lot, divide that amount by martinis. Since the standard computer keyboard is just like a typewriter, with a few extra buttons, learning the typing keyboard is a big plus. This can be accomplished with a manual checked out of your library, a borrowed typewriter, and fifteen minutes a day.

Another option is through the friendly Job Service Counselor with whom you've developed such comfortable rapport. This counselor can arrange computer training or formal training in many other areas of occupational skills. There may be a waiting list, and sometimes you may have to "qualify" through demonstration of financial need. If so, just having been out of work for a protracted period usually takes care of this requirement.

Finally, visit your blessed public library. This homey institution is such a dependable and indispensable agent for the serious job seeker that you'll find the entire next section devoted to its fantastic secrets. Many libraries have personal computers for public use. They also will probably have a do-it-yourself tutorial program you can run on the computer and teach yourself the "walkin'-around" moves and buzz words; erasing the mystique and enabling you to just say "yes, I am familiar with computers."

Time was when computer literacy meant mastery of complex and intricate programming languages. Not so any more. There are now hundreds of programs on the market that cover three basic work areas: word processing (what we used to call typing), data base (remember filing?), and spread sheet (bookkeeping). Every office or other work place will have invested in some commercial program covering these fields. These programs are designed to be learned quickly and easily; otherwise, employers won't buy them.

Employers will *expect* new workers to be familiar with computer operation, but they will usually be prepared to teach new employees the specific program they bought for their operation. Picture starting a job as a delivery person for UPS or Federal Express. You would be taught the routes and the billing procedures on the job. They would not, however, feel obliged to teach you how to drive the delivery truck!

Of course, training or retraining in any salable skill would be a valuable asset in a job search. However, the acquisition of computer familiarity is the quickest and easiest way to change your odds and to gain a fighting chance against "Mr. Clean," who's also sitting in that personnel office waiting room.

THE PUBLIC LIBRARY

The Public Library is the most valuable asset available to anyone beginning reentry into the job market.

How long has it been since you stepped into a library? A college term paper? It may date clear back to a grade school "get acquainted" field trip to the local public library. If it has been that long, your nose is in for a walk down memory lane. To me, libraries evoke a sudden recall of youth each time I walk through the threshold and the fragrance of a million books reaches my senses. Libraries still smell the same, all across the country. They're still relatively quiet, although there is no more shhhh!-ing. Business is now usually conducted in normal tones.

Newly sober job-seekers must get reintroduced to the public library and its services, because that is going to be your primary base of operations in town until you start on your new job. Its advantages cannot be duplicated; we'll enumerate a few, but you'll be able to find many more. Here are some of the ways libraries can help you with your job search:

1. They are open during the normal business hours you will have to be in town for interviews - including evenings and Saturdays.
2. They have listings of every company in the country by product, service and location.
3. They stock up-to-date trade journals so you can bone up on all the *in* subjects and buzz words that have developed while you were "at liberty."
4. All local and most national newspapers, complete with want ads, are delivered daily; and they are yours to read FREE.
5. There is a pay phone for making appointments for interviews.
6. They have sample employment tests for most occupations and job titles.
8. They also have the following top secret spy stuff on the company you're interest in:

a. full, correct company name
b. its address and ZIP
c. phone number of personnel office
d. names of all senior officers and board members
e. their titles and phone numbers
f. their home addresses
g. their wives' or husband's names
h. their previous positions or employers
i. their organizations and hobbies
j. what colleges they attended (and their fraternities, clubs and honor societies)
k. the corporate lineage of the company (who really owns it?)
l. what companies *it* controls
m. earnings and profits
n. major stockholders
o. product descriptions
p. number and types of employees
q. expansion plans
r. corporate gossip (planned moves, mergers, layoffs)
s. hiring policies
t. detailed descriptions of job specifications
u. inside intrigue (scandals, price wars, lawsuits, indictments for inside trading)
v. dangers lurking (products out of style, pending bankruptcy)
w. how to get there (city maps)

Besides helping you with your job search, libraries have many other wonderful qualities:

9. They are free; the only things requiring money are the pay phone, and coin-operated duplicating machines, electric typewriters, and personal computers.
10. They are warm in the winter, cool in the summer, and dry when it rains.
11. You can loaf in there as long as you wish and no one will question your presence.

12. No one will bug you; you'll get conversation only if you request information.
13. You can tell the librarian your name and where you are sitting, and she will give you brief phone messages.
14. They have excellent recreational reading and frequently show noon-time movies to watch with your brown-bag lunch.
15. There is a smoking room.
16. The toilets are clean.
17. *AND THEY DON'T SELL BOOZE!*

YOUR REFERENCES

What References?

Drinking alcoholics and other imperfect job seekers have many things in common. High on that list is fear of the unknown. They will worry themselves sick about bills, but leave an unopened letter from the loan company on the kitchen table——terrified to open it. They'll let the phone ring off the hook for fear that it may be a "bad" call. They always project the worst. While they were still employed, they would rather call in sick than honor a supervisor's invitation to " . . . stop by my office first thing in the morning."

Sound familiar? Even if an alcoholic or addict has gotten straight, those fears still hang on and get in the way of vocational recovery. One of the first things that comes to mind when you start your sober job search is, "How in the world can I explain what I've been doing these past several years? How can I possibly give working references? They'll surely check the references and call the places I've worked and then they'll find that I've been fired for being drunk or for poor performance or absenteeism, and then . . .?"

You're damn right they'll check your references and previous employment; and then they'll know something you don't know. They'll know *exactly* how your former employers are responding to inquiries of this sort. This is why you are going to adhere religiously to the following axiom:

ALWAYS CHECK YOUR OWN REFERENCES!

Why and How to Check Your Own References

Why in the world should everyone know more about us than we do? Usually substance abusers are the last to recognize that they have a problem. But this is a new chapter in your life. Just how do you find out what people are saying about you? We have a friend who is fond of saying that he is a member of the CIA—Catholic, Irish, and Alcoholic. Well, we're going to make like the real CIA. We're going to run a few little intelligence operations.

We have never worked with a recovering alcoholic or addict who has not been amazed at the simple logic of this firm little rule: **ALWAYS** CHECK YOUR OWN REFERENCES! And yet they would have never dreamt of doing it on their own. You may guess what a former employer will say about you, and you'll probably have a good idea what the former employer *should* say about you, but you will never know positively what is being said without checking it out. This is absolutely vital to vocational recovery. Ignorance is no longer bliss.

There are many reasons why former employers give work references that deviate from our idea of the truth. Some employers simply don't want the responsibility of making a public judgment on anything. They think, "The jerk screwed up here and I got rid of him. Now he's somebody else's headache. Good riddance." Then they answer the reference query with something bland, such as, " . . . worked here four months. Quit."

We were counseling an alcoholic technician, we'll call him E. Z. Duzzit, who had worked at Western Electric Corporation for four years before being fired for coming in drunk and picking a fight with his supervisor. On his applications for new jobs he had always omitted his time with Western Electric, convinced that their report on his drunk fiasco and subsequent firing would surely eliminate him from any further consideration. Instead, he had stretched the time he had worked at a small welding shop to cover this gap.

The owner of the welding shop had given him permission to do this, and told him that he hated to let him go, but they were in a slack period. He added encouragingly, "E.Z., Old Buddy, if there's anything I can do to help you, just let me know." E.Z. Duzzit finally joined AA and had been sober *and* unemployed for a year-and-a-half when he came to us for help. He had applied for work at dozens of places that he knew were hiring in areas of his qualifications, but he never got a nibble. Not a test, not an interview—nothing!

The first thing we did was to check his references. This is something he could and should have done himself at the very outset of his job search. It can be accomplished through any third person with a different name than yours. If you have a friend or relative with a business letterhead, all the better. The State Job Service Counselor can do the same thing, using her state letterhead, and modifying slightly the example below. The request is simple:

Dear Empoyer:
E.Z. Duzzit is being considered for a position in the electronics field, and he has reported employment with your company from January 1983 to June 1986. May we have a statement regarding Mr. Duzzit's service with you?
George J. Goodbuddy Associates

The response from Western Electric Personnel Department was prompt and brief. It consisted of a form post card.

"E.Z. Duzzit was employed with WE as an electronics technician between 1/29/83 and 6/4/86. Discharged. Reduction in force." (Stamped name of personnel chief)

Not a word about booze. Not a word about the fight with the supervisor. A year or so later I had the opportunity to meet E.Z. Duzzit's former WE supervisor at a National Alliance of Businessmen luncheon. We discussed E.Z.'s firing and it was obvious that the supervisor perceived any prejudicial termination as a time-consuming process involving voluminous paperwork, nerve-wracking hearings, and general hassle. So, when the personnel department told him that he was going to have to cut ten men off his shift, he saw an opportunity to get rid of a troublemaker.

Our letter to the welding shop was also an eye opener. The answer was a pencil-written note on the back of a requisition form:

> "If anyone hires that _____(censored) E.Z.Duzzit, he's NUTS! When he worked for me he was nothing but trouble."

And this was E.Z.'s prize reference! So now he knew as much as any prospective employer would, and could make the necessary adjustments.

Laundering Dirty References

Now just a cotton pickin' minute, Mr. Counselor! What about really hard cases, like mine? The only relevant employment I had was in a place like E.Z. Duzzit's welding shop, and I know they're going to pass out a 'kiss of death' reference. But it's absolutely the only reference I have and I'm thirty years old!

Now comes the time when you learn the practice of *practical humility.* You're going to learn how to launder your dirty references.

This is a model of a letter that would go to the welding shop owner and every other previous employer that your own reference check has shown probably will give potential employers disturbing reports on your service with them:

Dear Mr. Master,

I'm sure you are surprised to hear from me after all this time. Don't worry, I'm not asking for my old job back. Your action was certainly justified, and I would never ask you to retract it.

The purpose of this letter is to thank you for the understanding you showed me during the rough period I was going through when I worked for you. I'm sorry I couldn't

have been in your employ at some other time, but since
things have straightened out for me, I can truly say that I
would not have had the patience that you showed throughout my personal troubles. Please give my regards to the
gang in the shop.

Sincerely, E. Z. Duzzit

*NO WAY, Jose´! In a pig's eye will I write something like that.
I'll never grovel if I have to starve to death first!! So there.*
    That might be arranged. Many recovering alcoholics and their
families have suffered needless extra years of poverty and financial
dependence simply because of these hangovers from their drinking days: false pride and arrogance.
    Tailor this laundry letter to your particular situation, but do
not stray far from the wording or the brevity of the model above.
This letter has been field tested repeatedly and its success rate is
phenomenal. Sometimes the old employer even asks the contrite
writer to come back to work for him. Sometimes the edge comes
off the nasty reference check response. Something a little positive
always happens.
    And remember this: If you decide to launder your references,
you have absolutely nothing to lose! We have checked back with
employers on which this laundry letter has been used, and who
later "adjusted" the tone of their responses to reference checks. A
composite comment: "I knew he was jiving me, but I still couldn't
bring myself to give him a rotten reference after getting that damn
letter."
    Furthermore, you are not trying to get your former boss to lie
and say how wonderful you were. Your goal is only to get him to
modify his response: to remove totally negative comments and
leave you with something you can deal with at the job interview.
However corny this approach may sound, it works. If it is appropriate in your situation, swallow your pride (instead of a drink)
and give it an honest shot. Another reminder. You must always
recheck your references again after sending the laundry letter to
see exactly what is going to be sent to the prospective employers.

Don't Confess

You will notice that alcoholism, drug addiction, or jail time is not mentioned in the laundry letter. Nonalcoholics are always quick to attribute drinking or drugging to other factors—home conditions, financial binds, health problems—rather than the other way around. This is fine. Just let that misconception stand; it saves much explaining.

A confession of chemical addiction in a two-paragraph letter to a former employer may be a surprise to him. And, since he hasn't been attending all these educational counseling sessions with you, or heard my lectures on the joys of hiring recovered alcoholics, the revelation that this lazy and unreliable s.o.b. was *also* drinking and drugging will definitely not produce a positive effect. The letter from E. Z. Duzzit's welding shop boss after receiving such a confessional might well be changed as follows:

"If anyone hires that *drunken* E.Z.Duzzit, he's nuts"

Alternate Reference Sources

Please Note! Another useful method of sidestepping a potentially bad reference is by directing the referral to a friendly supervisor. Employers will usually address reference checks exactly the way they are written on the application or résumé. If there is an office manager or supervisor that can be singled out as possibly having a residual liking for you or one who may be ignorant of your aberrant behavior, call or write to this person at his home, and ask if you can use him as a reference.

This may have been someone you worked for in another department before you started getting stupid and got canned, or simply someone you think you can trust. It may be someone a step below or above the person who was *technically* your immediate supervisor. If approval is received, the reference is then listed as:

"XYZ Corporation, Attention: Nestor Niceguy; Manager, Accounts Receivable."

Nestor can then answer the query by confirming dates of employment and attesting to your knowledge and ability. *Then this reference must be tested, even though you've set it up.* You must know exactly what is being told to prospective employers, no matter how good a friend Nestor Niceguy may be.

4

FACING
THE APPLICATION FORM

Why does the Employment Application Form frighten you so? This routine little blank form strikes as strong a chord of fear in the alcoholic applicant for employment as does the interview itself.

This piece of paper is an instrument of torture with which the employer attempts to force everyone into a mold designed for Mr. and Ms. Clean, and it fits you, the imperfect job seeker, like a bloody iron maiden. As the mold tightens, any stray bits and pieces that don't fit will stick out and flag you as "different." Personnel people don't want "different" employees. All "different" people are potential personnel problems. This is the prime reason for my precautionary discussion of the *confessional.*

When you walk into a company's employment office—whether you have an interview appointment, referral from the Job Service, or just came in cold off the street on a hunch—there are many things you don't know. You probably don't know if you will be interviewed by a man or a woman. You aren't sure whether he or she will be Caucasian, African-American, Hispanic, Oriental, or Eskimo. You wonder if the interviewer will really be conversant in the job you're shooting for or just a "personnel type." You don't know if you'll be ushered right in or be made to cool your heels for an hour.

There really is only one thing that you are absolutely sure of: You will be asked to fill out an application form.

This application will become part of the permanent personnel file if you're hired, so it must not be entrusted to a panicky, guilt-ridden *ad lib* amateurish snow job. You *know* you're going to have to fill out an application form—dozens of them, if you're conducting a really serious job search. You know it is an important facet of your job search, and you know, or will know, what information you will be asked to supply. This document must be prepared in advance with much more care than your résumé, as it is many times more important than the overrated résumé.

WHAT'S ON THE APPLICATION FORM?

Most old application forms (and many still in use) were designed not to fit the applicant to the job, but to find out as much personal information as possible.

Many long years ago when I was working as a private investigator, one of the first calls I would make would be to my subject's former employer. There, on the original application card in the personnel office would be the life history of the subject and all of his or her family, plus health record, driving record, what church the person belonged to, how much money was owed (and to whom), hobbies, likes and dislikes, organizations belonged to (and degree of participation), the extent of traveling (when and where and for what purpose), social contacts ("List five close, personal friends not related to you"), and so on.

All this is changing. Please note that I say *changing*, not that it *has* changed. The trend of the state and federal governments and their court systems has been, in recent years, to reflect the urgent desire of their constituency to (1) protect privacy, and (2) confine job specifications to those with proven application to the job.

Job applications got out of hand three ways. Some employers were simply terribly nosey and figured they were entitled to know *everything* about prospective employees. Others had deeply ingrained prejudices and were convinced they needed this information to weed out potential troublemakers and poor performers. They would devise intricate formulas assigning points to each answer on the questionnaire, with minus numbers for "bad" answers. Finally, by far the largest percentage of employers simply ordered application forms from their printer or from a supply house. To satisfy the most conditions of employment for the most customers, generic forms were designed to be all-encompassing, and therefore flexible.

Regulatory agencies routinely shoot down improper application questions every day. Many of these decisions have been tested in court, upheld, and become part of the body of case law on this subject. Most employers, especially the larger ones and those holding federal contracts, have voluntarily corrected their application forms to eliminate everything except the purely job-related questions.

The movement for fair application forms started as a civil rights measure to improve the lot of African-Americans who had been systematically excluded from voting through complicated and largely irrelevant questions. This was extended to include equal employment opportunity, and protected classes were increased to include other minorities, women, religious groups, the young, the old, veterans, handicapped workers and, in some states, homosexuals.

As each law is written to add another protected class, the employer is faced with more "shall not" clauses to comply with in preparation of his application forms. To cope with this, most intelligent and far-sighted employers have already revised their applications in anticipation of future laws that will be aimed at assuring that only questions directly relating to any applicant's ability to do the job may be answered.

The government's watchdog agency, the Equal Employment Opportunity Commission, has filed thousands of suits across the country in the past decade, and some determinations important to recovering alcoholics are noted. For example, an employer cannot ask:

- With whom you are living (but may request a name of someone so as to contact you)

- Irrelevant education
- Irrelevant licenses
- Date of birth (unless over 65, for pension purposes; they also may ask if the applicant is over 18)
- Questions on debts or charge accounts
- Questions on garnishments
- Questions about arrests or confinements (They may ask about convictions, but this cannot be used as the sole basis for disqualification unless directly related to the job—such as a former child molester applying to work in a day care center or an ex-embezzler who needs bonding.)
- And, they cannot force you to take a lie detector test.

Please remember that these are only a few of the determinations made by EEOC at the time of this writing. Also remember that these determinations were results of *lawsuits*. Don't be surprised if a potential employer asks you everything on this list and much more.

Discrimination and the Employment Application

There are additional danger areas in application filing of which you should be aware. Employers are usually upheld when challenged for discharging someone after learning that they lied on their application. Exceptions are when it can be shown that the employer probably would have *illegally* rejected you had you answered correctly. Example: An employer asks on an application, "Do you have an honorable discharge from the military service?" If an applicant answers untruthfully and is later fired for lying, he probably would win a reinstatement suit if he could show that he had knowledge that the employer refused to hire anyone with less than honorable discharges.

Also, falsification of federal job applications (SF 171) is illegal; however, you may rest assured that there are no illegal questions on that form.

I suspect that you really don't have time for crusades right now. It should be your intention to obtain a job *without* taking the employer to court. Nevertheless, if you come across blatant disregard of the antidiscriminatory hiring trend in federal and state statutes, you may decide it is your duty to blow the whistle. Please give this action some careful study, however, before you decide to sacrifice yourself on the altar of social progress. An anonymous call or letter to the EEOC might be more appropriate unless you have totally written this employer off.

Also, these rulings can change periodically, and will be affected by court decisions and state laws governing employment rights. If you have some heavy health or legal problems in your background, you should contact the EEOC (2401 E Street NW; Washington, DC 20507). These people will be able to give you an up-to-date briefing on your rights under current state law, along with the employer's responsibilities.

But let's presume from here on out, that your primary function is to find a job, not to right all of the injustices in the field of personnel acquisition. We hope you will be able to avoid litigation for two reasons: (a) It takes time. All compliance agencies have a backlog of cases, and even after yours comes up, you can look forward to many more months of investigation and conciliation hearings; and, (b) Unless you are talking about a very large corporation where one can be absorbed and forgotten immediately after hire, it isn't going to be much fun to work for a boss who was forced to employ you.

Should You Reveal Your Alcoholism?

A few years ago I had a discussion with a business executive regarding the pros and cons of full disclosure of past substance abuse by recovered alcoholics. He strongly objected to my advising recovered alcoholics to avoid unnecessary confessionals of past abuse.

He cited an example of a man he had interviewed for an executive position who had withheld information about past abuse of alcohol. He hired him, and the man got drunk and became an expensive embarrassment to the firm. I asked if he would have hired the applicant had he confessed his history of alcoholism. Of course, he would not have. "But," he continued, ". . . you're teaching alcoholics to lie."

I find the very thought of teaching an active alcoholic to lie on a par with teaching a baby to suck a nipple. Of course, we don't recommend lying to an employer; that is an intimate decision to be made by the job seeker.

If you have planned to disguise or "lose" part of your past on application forms, and you honestly shared this intent with your counselor, you probably watched him try to screw himself into his seat. This is a very touchy subject with counselors.

The following is an exerpt from a talk I gave to a group of counselors several years ago:

> *At times we may be lulled into thinking that we are dealing with children. But these are people who have been coping and surviving in a real world for years. Not the real world of productive participation in society, but a very real, and very mean world, nevertheless. They have been making critical and desperate decisions for years. They will continue to make decisions, for better or worse, as the occasions arise.*
>
> *Most of you will be counseling alcoholics and addicts— the most accomplished liars on earth (when actively into their addictions.) But we have known many job seekers who, in the rainbow glow of their first year of sobriety, have blown interview after interview by proudly announcing to everyone that they are alcoholics. They felt better physically and mentally than they had in years. Furthermore, they were so exalted in the knowledge that they had a disease that could be arrested, and were not moral lepers or insane monsters, that they felt they had to spread the gospel. Believe me, the world of employment is not ready for this!*
>
> *If you are not aware of these axioms, be aware of them now!*
>
> *1. Most recovered job seekers will be faced with critical questions regarding their past behavior at some time during their job search.*
> *2. All things being equal, a personnel interviewer will select a nonadmitting alcoholic or user over ones who proudly and loudly proclaim their past addiction.*

3. *Faced with direct questions, job seekers will make that extremely important decision regarding full confession or withholding of certain derogatory information concerning substance abuse, and they'll make it with or without your input.*
4. *This very personal decision should be made only after careful deliberation, in the calm of their home, or in your office, and not spontaneously in the heat of an employment interview.*

The world of business is not ready for unwarranted full and open disclosure of past intemperances. Applicants may have only a few minutes to sell themselves through their application forms and job interview responses. They don't have time to give the employer a four-year graduate course on the disease concept of alcoholism!

If your clients come to you with the firm and final decision that they intend to omit or tailor their answers on a portion of an application for employment, it is your duty to ensure that they have a full grasp of the following admonitions. Any falsification on an application, no matter how minor:

- *Must be done as a last resort, not as a convenience, and only after a studied determination that they have no chance without doing this.*
- *Must be made with full recognition of the risk involved. Walk through a "worst possible scenario" with them, and force them to enumerate what would happen if their little deception "blew." Make sure they are willing to accept this as worthy of the risk.*
- *Should be backstopped if necessary, but without an elaborate cover story.*
- *Must NEVER, NEVER, NEVER be volunteered!*

When it comes to discussions of total honesty in job search, a counselor may feel like parents who plead with their child to practice abstinence, but reluctantly include birth control and AIDS protection in the discourse. Fabrication is a tactic you may decide you have to plan for but hope you'll never have to use. If it is ever your decision to use it, you must understand that it is only an emergency measure in the game of survival——sort of like the ejection seat on a jet plane.

Government job search is a different matter, in that truthful response on their applications is compelled by statute. However, you will find that government application forms and interviews are extremely kind to the recovered alcoholic who opts against the gratuitous confessional. Federal and state recruitment techniques have been carefully honed in recent years to protect the privacy and rights of the applicant.

If you have made the irrevocable decision to make "adjustments" in your personal history, don't even consider using this fiction if it isn't absolutely necessary. I know of several job hunters who had socially nasty episodes in their lives around which they had carefully designed believable cover stories. When neither the application form nor the interviewer gave them an opportunity to explain away the time they spent in the slammer or the Home For The Bewildered, they couldn't see wasting the creativity that went into their plot.

"By the way, I suppose you're wondering why I wasn't working during 1984. Well, you see, I was taking care of my sick aunt and writing a book."

The interviewer wasn't wondering before, but she sure is now!

A PRACTICAL JOB APPLICATION EXERCISE

Let's role-play for a moment, and suppose that you are an alcoholic named E. Z. Duzzit, and you are trying to reenter the job market as a drafter. You really messed up the last few years of your drinking. You were hospitalized several times for alcoholism. You were frequently arrested for disorderly conduct and intoxication and once for atrocious assault and battery. You're sober now, and faced with a job search that will inevitably involve applications requiring responses in those areas.

The first matter to consider is good intelligence. Not "IQ" intelligence, but CIA-type intelligence. You *must* know more about your present situation than anyone else knows *or can find out.*

Exceptions to the 'Don't Confess' Rule

Obviously no company who knew about the trouble you've gotten into through alcohol would hire you. Oh, really? "Obviously" is a cop-out word used by someone trying to avoid hard investigation. There are a few companies who have very progressive programs regarding alcoholism, and who welcome recovered alcoholics (provided they have evidence of their sincerity and a favorable prognosis).

Generally, unemployed alcoholics and drug addicts are unemployed because of their addictions. While they will have job search obstacles related to residual addictive personality traits, their ability to perform adequately on the job usually rebounds as a normal bonus of sobriety.

As employers of successfully recovered alcoholics will testify, their performance frequently surpasses anything they may have dreamt of before their acceptance of their disease. One hard-nosed corporate executive told me that every sober alcoholic involved in a permanent recovery program was worth 1.6 units of personnel when measured on dependability, and quantity and quality of work.

But these companies are as scarce as hen's teeth and must be carefully ferreted out. If you are a member of AA, you could have your Intergroup representative check with their Industrial Relations Committee. As you know, AA is not an employment agency. All you will be looking for are some names of firms with a policy of understanding and reception of recovering alcoholics.

Now, if there is such a rare bird in your vicinity, make sure this policy extends down to the personnel office. We've known many corporations with recovered alcoholics on their boards of directors who contribute heavily of their time and money to matters involving alcoholism rehabilitation, but whose personnel departments operate with insensitivity. Check this out very carefully before you commit yourself. Remember, we're talking about an *exception* to the *Don't Confess* rule.

Medical References

If you have a family doctor who has treated you during your active alcoholism and is aware of your recovery, you may wish to have a candid talk with him or her about the subject of medical references. Ask how the doctor would reply if a potential employer asked about your health. What would the hospital reply if asked for an evaluation? You might mention to the doctor that you are anxious to get back to work and start paying off your bills (including the doctor's). Then, whatever answer you receive, *check it out!*

There is the story of the shopkeeper who thought it was time to teach his eight-year-old son the rudiments of business so he could take over the store some day. He stood him up on the counter and said, "Now, just close your eyes and fall backwards into my arms. Daddy will catch you." As the little boy closed his eyes and let himself fall, his daddy stepped out of the way and let him hit the floor with a bruising thud. Then he called out over the child's wails, "That's the first lesson. Don't trust *anyone.*"

We certainly don't want to add paranoia to all of your other problems, but it is absolutely imperative that you always know *exactly* what friend and opponent alike are saying about you when your job search is at stake. Check your doctor out the same way you checked out your own references. Get a friend or your Job Service counselor to write a letter similar to the one below:

Medical Administrator
Central County Hospital
Cartersville, Indiana

Dear Director:

E.Z.Duzzit is being considered for employment by our firm (or through our Agency) in the position of drafter. Because the job may entail working in remote locations, we have asked for a medical reference and he has provided the attached signed medical release for that purpose. As a means of further identification, Mr. Duzzit was treated at your hospital between June 6, 1987 and August 8, 1987, and was under the care of Dr. Victor Vallium.

In addition to a statement regarding this treatment and prognosis, we would appreciate any comment regarding physical limitations that should be considered in his placement.

Sincerely,
Kenneth M. Goodbuddy

This would, of course, be accompanied by a slip stating the following:

I hereby authorize the Central County Hospital to release medical information concerning me to Kenneth Goodbuddy.

(Signed) - E. Z. Duzzit

Job Service counselors are accustomed to making similar routine requests as "Physcaps" or "Psycaps," which simply mean physical or psychological capability reports. These really aren't going to tell you what you want to know, as the hospitals and doctors will naturally tend to be more open and honest with a counselor who is bound by the laws and ethics of confidentiality and who intends to use the information for professional vocational guidance.

Unless the Job Service counselor completely understands what you are trying to accomplish by this little "intelligence operation," best use someone else. Remember, as long as replies will get delivered, the requester's name isn't important. Your wife's sister, Lillian Ann Lovable, can suddenly become L. A. Lovable Associates for this exercise.

Now you will find out whether the doctor and hospital are telling the world that you were treated for alcoholism, or acute pancreatitis or gastroenteritis, or some other fancy nickname for the disease. The employer's questions for which you are preparing probably will not appear in the initial application, but in the medical questionnaire you will fill out just before the company physical. If it looks as if you are going to get a lousy report, you will have to decide whether to put that part of your past in the closet.

Everyone faced with this problem makes that decision. Since matters of jeopardy in group health plans might be involved, this becomes a highly personal decision but a decision you will make, nevertheless. All I can do at this point is to repeat the admonition to make your decision beforehand, after cool, calculated reflection of all aspects of the situation, and *not* in the sweat and panic of the company personnel office.

If, after considering all alternatives, you feel that you would not get the job with a total disclosure of your health history, your choices boil down to (1) baring all and letting them do with you what they will, (2) quietly picking up your briefcase and coat and ducking out the door, or (3) keeping certain past health problems to yourself.

Presuming you are applying for a job in the private sector, an employer would have to run his own massive intelligence operation to check all possible hospital and treatment centers, then obtain confidential medical information without your written consent. If your alcoholism has left no permanent damage to your body that would be important to have recorded in company or insurance records, you may have decided to just check "no" to those questions that would require long explanations of hospital stays for alcoholism related disorders.

Arrest Records

Similarly, when dealing with arrest records, a good intelligence project is most important. The fact that questions about arrest records are usually improper, and that convictions can be used only to determine "*bona fide* occupational qualifications" (shortened to BFOQ by the Equal Employment Opportunity Commission), is little comfort if the questions blatantly appear on the questionnaire of a firm in which you are interested. This might not be the proper time to blow the whistle on those noncomplying employers.

On the other hand, we have seen such "adjustments" made by counselors for individual clients that later benefitted many of them. One veteran we were working with was particularly interested in three major companies in the area. Unfortunately, he had an arrest record a mile long for alcoholism-related offenses, punctuated by a couple of convictions. We requested and obtained copies of application forms from these companies for "training purposes." You can do this, or have anyone walk into the company employment office, ask for an application blank, and walk out.

In this instance, we reviewed the questions, and, indeed, there were items that would distress our friend. "Have you ever been arrested? Please itemize incidents, including details of convictions, sentence, present parole or probationary status." These were referred to an attorney in EEOC, who called the personnel officer of the corporation. She explained that since the jobs for which the form was being used did not involve bonding, details of convictions were not BFOQ (*bona fide* occupational requirements), and questions about arrests were simply improper. The director of personnel thanked her for the information, and when our friend went back to apply for a job, those troubling items were carefully obliterated with black marker on all applications.

But let's assume that this neat and tidy gimmick is not appropriate for you, E. Z. Duzzit. Your first task is to attempt to find out what information is available to employers in the way of police record checks. Now wouldn't it be simple to call the police and ask them how much information they give out to employers on request? No, not unless you have a very close buddy or relative in the police records branch. A question such as this will spook them.

We have called police administration offices in several cities asking for just that general information, and were told how carefully they protected the rights of individuals who had been arrested and later released or acquitted. Then a few days later, we posed as an employer and requested record checks on a couple of people with whom we were working. The police pulled the file and gave us the entire rap sheet, including nonconvictions and convictions alike.

Furthermore, many companies use off-duty police officers as part-time security guards, and it is routine for them to have the guard obtain this information. Your job is to find out exactly what an employer could find out.

Your Job Service counselor, a colleague, or you, yourself (if you've attained enough sober *chutzpah* yet) can call or write the local police records branch. "I'm considering hiring E.Z. Duzzit and I want to check his police record." Except for juvenile offenses, convictions are matters of public record. Even in these cases, some record clerks require that the individual requesting the information either come down in person or send a certified check to cover duplication and mailing of the record.

Consider discussing this with your Legal Aid Society or the attorney representing your institution, and the American Civil Liberties Union in your city or state capital. If you have been represented by an attorney during your troubles and are still on good terms with him or her, you may want to obtain professional advice on this matter. Knowing the local situation, your lawyer may have good ideas for slowing or impeding the flow of derogatory information on you. If you were arrested and subsequently acquitted, the expunging of your record should definitely be explored.

I possess neither the competence nor authority to give legal advice that might be applicable to anyone's particular situation. However, here are a few actual examples of how other recovering alcoholics have gotten around the police record roadblock, and they are shared only with the hope they may excite your ingenuity.

The drafter mentioned earlier in this chapter had passed up several job interviews because the application form asked about arrest records. That this may or may not have been a proper question is immaterial——there it was——and when he saw it he either checked "yes" and added the gory details in the "remarks" section as *ordered* by the piece of paper, or he just walked out of the office without finishing the form. In either case, he eliminated himself for every job opening that threw that damning question at him.

In the jurisdiction where he resided, "atrocious assault and battery" is a serious crime that would be charged by a grand jury after which the accused would be brought to trial. Our drafter had beaten up a friend in a bar brawl on a Friday night. He was taken to jail, told he was being booked for atrocious assault and battery, and was brought before the judge the following Monday. There he was given a scolding and sent home.

We requested a police check for employment purposes under our letterhead, and received the response "no record." This was something he could have done himself at the onset of his job search. The only derogatory information available to any potential employer was what he *himself* had volunteered.

Nancy Newstart had served five days of a sixty-day sentence for drunk driving and had her license revoked for one year. Although she had held several jobs while living in the state where this took place, they were of short duration, and she decided that they wouldn't be crucial to her work history. She eliminated all references to residence or work in that state on her application form and buried that part of her life.

Please be aware that if Nancy had applied for a job with the federal government or most law enforcement agencies, they would have had access to a national computerized listing of all arrests going back to approximately 1963. The accuracy of this check, called the NCIC, depends on the quality and quantity of input from all law enforcement entities in the fifty states. Nevertheless, it is pretty darn accurate, and any decision to ignore or rewrite history should be confined to job search in the private sector.

Remembering that all examples in this area are isolated, let's look at another actual situation handled by an applicant we'll call Karl Kool. Karl was applying for work in the same community where he had been in trouble, and it was necessary to finesse part of the worrisome "offenses" question. He left blank the space designed for the answer to arrest questions, and turned in the form.

When he was called for his interview, the personnel officer went over the application card, asking polite questions about this or that town where he had lived or worked. When she came to the question on arrests, she smiled sweetly, and said, "Mr. Kool, I notice you've left this item blank. Would you care to discuss it?" He looked her in the eye, smiled back, and said, "As you know,

that is an illegal question unless bonding is a previously established requisite of the position. Since that isn't the case here, I
assumed that it didn't apply to me. If you insist on having all the
blanks filled in, you can just write 'none' there."

Well, Karl got the job, although he had discovered through
his own investigations that his record was easily obtainable by
employers in that town, and that this employer routinely checked
police records. We can only assume that his pointing out the
impropriety of the question caused the company to skip the record
check, at least in his case. If at some time his record came to light,
Karl reasoned, and someone tried to burn him for falsifying his
application, the "none" was obviously written in by another hand.

Juan Dey was looking for work in the same medium-sized city
where he had gotten into jam after jam through the abuse of
alcohol. His parish priest approached the police chaplain and told
him that Juan was sober now, but his record would surely make
it rough to find a job. While he didn't want to suggest any
interference with the process, he would consider it a personal
favor if he could be notified whenever derogatory information on
Juan was supplied to an employer. We don't know what effect this
approach had on subsequent events, but Juan's luck suddenly
changed and the good Father was never notified of passage of
damaging information.

As we say in computerland, "Don't Confess" is still the default
drive, and the next story doesn't change that realism. Harry
Holloleg had a reputation throughout the industry as the "playboy
plumber." The normal conversation opener at the local barbershop
was "I see Harry made the paper again."

His escapades with the bottle and in the courts were very much
public knowledge. He had lost his plumbing business and, after he
attained sobriety, decided it would be best for his continuing
recovery if he had a steady job with regular hours. He went to the
National Alliance of Businessmen, an organization that is dedicated to placement of disadvantaged, handicapped, veterans, and
ex-offenders. He obtained a list of member companies who had
pledged to support this program by hiring some workers from
each of these groups. Harry then wrote to the president of each
company as follows:

Dear Mr. Rotary,

I am writing to you because of my knowledge of your dedication to the principles of the National Alliance of Businessmen. As a business man you are aware that you will never be able to obtain a plumbing maintenance man of my experience and talent for the $25,000 at which I am willing to start.

Although I no longer drink, my past problem has enabled me to fulfill the legal definition of disadvantaged, handicapped, and ex-offender. As I am also a veteran, I am offering you my skill at a bargain price, plus four tallies toward your pledge to the NAB.

Since I am probably one of the few employees you will have who does not drink, I'm also offering a unique degree of reliability and dependability. My résumé is enclosed. I will call you Wednesday morning if I don't hear from you sooner.

Sincerely

Harry Holloleg

The purpose of these examples is not to give you a model to copy, but to illustrate how individual recovering alcoholics, just like you, managed to get over this very real obstacle by ingenious applications of the following suggestions to their personal situations. You should be satisfied that you:

1. Know *exactly* what the police have on record about you.
2. Know *precisely* what is entailed in getting a record check in your particular locality. (Convictions only? Arrests, too? Other details?)
3. Have attempted to learn if your target company routinely makes police checks.
4. Understand that you must *always* make your decision about what to put on an application, what to leave out, and so on, at home and *not* in the pressure and panic of the personnel office.

5. Recognize that any decision to omit or fabricate portions of your work or personal history must be made only after careful consideration of all angles, and never as a short cut or convenience. If there is a risk involved, it must be a calculated risk. And, this decision must not be made in a casual or flippant manner.

THE HONESTY TEST

Preemployment "honesty" testing has now replaced the polygraph, or "lie detector," as a screening device. Employee theft of goods and ideas was recognized as a major business problem during the 1970s and 1980s, and polygraph operation became a prestige industry. When the Supreme Court declared the polygraph to be an unfair prerequisite for employment, businesses readily found a handier, quicker, less expensive, and probably less reliable substitute: the employee honesty prediction test. You should understand the philosophy and practical application of this widely used test.

Typically, the applicant is given a long written test, usually multiple choice. A time limit for completion adds a degree of stress. Many questions will seem totally irrelevant to honesty. This is because they *are* irrelevant, and are merely used to upholster the critical questions, throwing the applicant off guard. The questions that will actually be scored will run the gamut of apparently obvious to gray areas that will give the applicant problems.

Imagine answering the following questions with one of the following responses. You are allowed to check only one answer, and no explanations are permitted:

(a) Never
(b) Seldom
(c) Rarely
(d) Only under desperate circumstances

• Would you steal a $5000 computer from your employer?

- Have you ever taken a used pencil home from work?
- If you needed a paper clip for personal use, would you take one from the office?
- Have you ever falsified a travel voucher?
- If you suspected a friend and co-worker of stealing, would you refrain from reporting her to security?
- Have you ever used the company telephone to make an important personal call?
- Have you ever taken tools from work for home use?
- When wrapping a personal package during your break, would you use office tape and staples?
- Would you use the company gas pump to fill your personal car?
- Have you *ever* done small personal chores on company time?
- Have you ever been fired for stealing?

Questions similar to the above, couched in many ways, may go on for several pages. The applicant who is trying to be super-honest, whether by personal conviction or instruction from a counselor, probably will blow this type of test. Unfortunately, the machine that will grade this preemployment honesty prediction exam doesn't give a damn about one's principles or those of the counselor.

The logic behind these tests is really quite simple. A dishonest applicant would steal a computer, tools, and gas. But he knows the employer doesn't want to hear that. So he'll check *"never"* on those blatant questions. But he also knows that everyone steals time and pens, and figures the employer knows this, too. So, to appear honest, he will check (b), (c), or (d) for those questions.

On the other hand, reckons the cunning test composer, the honest applicant would never even think of stealing a computer or tools. Of course, he might walk out with a pen or a half-used pad of paper to work on his income tax at home, but he knows the employer doesn't want to hear that. He recognizes this to be wrong, is ashamed of his past delinquencies in that regard, and surmises such an admission of gross immorality would preclude his acceptance for employment. So he puts down *"never"* on all or ninety-nine percent of his responses.

Unfair as this may seem, this system works out to be statistically accurate. Many companies have participated in blind tests of these exams. Applicants were given the exams by the testing agency, and the results were not revealed to the employers. A year later, the test scores of employees who were fired for theft or other dishonesty were pulled out. Almost without exception, those dishonest employees would have been screened out by the exam.

Unfortunately, fine folks who *didn't* steal anything also would have been screened out by this test. The testing firms counter by suggesting that they only measured the ones that got caught. The others that would have been wiped out at the hiring desk *might* have stolen stuff and not gotten caught, or they might steal something next year.

If you take one of these honesty prediction tests, you are not talking to your priest, and you're not at an AA or NA meeting. You are talking to a damn machine that wants to see *Never, Never, Never, Never, ad infinitum.*

5

POSITIONING:

BETTER ODDS FOR YOUR APPLICATION

Crib sheets, which we all remember by various names from school exam times, will instill confidence, eliminate panicky guesses, and improve the odds of being hired.

CRIB SHEETS

The crib you will prepare before you make your first trip to the company employment office is for a much more important examination than you ever had in school, and it's perfectly legitimate. It must be done carefully at home or at the library, with painstaking care, and it is *not* optional.

The first draft of your crib will be done on regular paper, but the final copy will be carefully designed to fit your wallet when folded once, lengthwise. You can use as many sheets as you need, but you should number the items and permanently secure the pages in proper order with a staple. The crib should be typed, if possible, otherwise printed in indelible ink and a fine-point pen.

Listed below you will find items that may be expected to appear on application forms for both private sector and civil service employment. Some questions border on being improper under current interpretations of the law, but, as I mentioned earlier, these questions still appear. It is your mission to get a job, not to become the great immortal application-blank Lone Ranger.

You should not try to commit any of these matters to memory. You'd be surprised what one will forget under pressure. We've seen people filling out applications who asked to use the phone so they could check with their spouse about their ZIP code or the spelling of their street name, and then had to ask for the phone book!

Name

Always put last name first if so directed. Surnames should be printed in capital letters and given names in small letters. This is especially important if the surname is also a common given name, i.e., ELLIOTT, Carter E. (Being mis-alphabetized is a frustration I've endured all my life.) Being so familiar with our names, we cannot understand why the spelling would not be immediately recognizable to everyone. However, we know of many applicants who were not called in for interviews because of illegible names. You should practice printing your name in block letters until you are satisfied there is no chance of misinterpreting the spelling. Absolutely no fancy flourishes.

Address

I recommend carrying two pens on a job hunt. One should be a fine ball point, sometimes called a bookkeeping point, for use in the inadequate space usually provided for address information. The wider point pen, such as a *Flair*, is useful in writing longer statements. *It also dresses up shaky penmanship.*

The address should always be complete, including apartment number and ZIP code. Many companies have a firm rule against mail going out without a ZIP code. If a clerk is sending out call-in cards to fifty applicants for interviews, she is going to pick the first fifty that have legible names, addresses, and ZIP codes, because ZIPs are a pain to look up in the directory. If you are living with your sister, you should put "c/o Sarah G. Sibling" as an integral part of the address. Otherwise a helpful new mail carrier might assume a letter to you was misaddressed, and return it.

If you are living in a hotel frequented by drifters, try to arrange for a mailing address. This is especially important if you are conducting your job search from jail, a hospital, or a halfway house. Even innocent residence at a YMCA attaches a stigma to any job seeker over college age. If you have no friends or relatives in the immediate area for address purposes, you can subtly disguise your quarters: "Apartment 503; 600 Broad Street, Newark, NJ 07102" is a room at the Newark "Y."

One recovering alcoholic used an impressive address similar to this: "Donald D. Dry, c/o Martin Wiseman Associates; Suite 12B, Box 1506, Somewhere, MO 55555." Box 1506 was the post office box of the Veterans Hospital; Suite 12B was the Psychiatric Ward, and Martin Wiseman was his ward psychiatrist.

CAUTION! Don't go overboard on this and jeopardize delivery of your mail. You must keep an accurate record of all places you have applied for work, and inform them by mail, telephone, in person, or all three every time you change your address. This also serves the function of causing the employer to pull out your application and correct the address. Hopefully this means taking another look at the form in the process; it also reminds the employer of your continued interest in the position.

A final word on addresses. Over the years I have participated in many mass call-ins by employers, by which large groups of job applicants are summoned to report for interviews or physicals. This usually happened when a new shift opened or a new project was launched. Inevitably, over fifteen percent of the call-in cards would be returned, stamped by the post office "Addressee Unknown."

We never knew if they forgot their street number when they filled out the application, neglected to tell a friend they were going to use his address, just made the whole thing up to fill in a dull day, or were kidnapped by visitors from outer space. We never heard from that fifteen percent again——and they never heard from us.

Phone Number

Include the area code, even when applying to a local firm. Applications are sometimes sent to a home office in a distant city for processing and review, or shared with another company who may need personnel of your type. If you are living alone, or with someone who works, always add the number of a relative or friend who will take messages. Then you must make sure that *every* member of that person's family is aware that you are using the number. Add the word "message" after the number on the application. The crib sheet will note: "555-344-7766/message George and Sarah Goodbuddy before 3 p.m."

Refrain from using public places as message drops; and *never* use a bar.

Birth Date

This is not the place to fudge. Unless you can safely carve fifteen years off your age, it won't make any difference and won't be worth the risk. Furthermore, alcoholics usually look their age. At least!

Social Security Number

Put this on the crib sheet; you might have a mental block. Furthermore, if you are hired and you have one digit wrong on your Social Security Number, all of your hard-earned pension contributions will go to someone else's account!

Position Applying For

This may not be appropriate for entry in your permanent crib sheet because you probably will be applying to many companies for several different types of positions. Nevertheless, you must learn to expect this question and know what you intend to write *before* you leave home. This should be kept as general and flexible as possible, remembering that this question is a favorite among low-level personnel people for screening applicants *out* of further consideration. Answers such as "Production," "Office," "Sales," "Warehouse,"or "Laboratory" are all acceptable. *"Anything" is not.*

Lowest Pay You Will Accept

You must not let this one take you by surprise. It will almost *always* be asked in one way or another, either on the application form or at the job interview. An interviewer can very quickly learn how much an applicant knows about the job for which he is applying by simply asking "What is the minimum salary you would accept?" A stammering, "Well, of course, that depends on the job," or, "I'll take anything if it has a future," shows little research by the applicant. Chances are you have no idea what the job should pay, and you really *would* take "anything" just to get your foot in the door.

If you don't know the fair salary for the target job, begin with the state government. Every state has a bureau that deals with wage standards. They will be under the Department of Labor, Labor and Industry, Employment Commission, or Human Resources, and will have representatives in most large cities. Ask your Job Service Counselor for the name, location, and phone number of the nearest office, probably called the Prevailing Wage Office. Its function is to collate all reported salaries and wages being paid for specific occupations in the state and to supply current averages and ranges for each area.

This office also will be able to give you comparative wages for surrounding states. Always ask for both entry level and journey-man ranges. You may even be able to find out what a particular company is paying now. Most companies try to keep the pay ranges of their white-collar employees private so as to have greater freedom in giving incentive awards and job assignment. Nevertheless, you *must* be able to frame your acceptable starting wage or salary within reasonable limits.

A recovering alcoholic, who lost a professional career during his drinking, began a diligent job search, confident that he could work his way up the ladder once he got his foot in the door. Unfortunately, his perfectionist/inferiority complex took charge and he accepted the first job that was offered. He subconsciously feared taking a chance on future rejection and rationalized that a bird in the hand . . ..

The job was in the neighboring town and paid the minimum wage at the time ($3.25 per hour) for extruder operation in a plastics plant. It had been twenty years since he had worked for an hourly wage and that was for two dollars an hour, so this sounded about right. But his first check came to only $110.50 after deductions. He owed $65 a week child support and $40 room rent, and the bus fare to and from work was a dollar a day. This meant working overtime, and then double time.

It was a filthy job, and by the time he was scrubbed up, he was too worn out to continue his job search. The inevitable happened. The night shift cut out his vital AA meetings, and one day he got too hungry, angry, lonely, and tired, and he picked up a drink.

A little advance planning would have shown him that he simply couldn't hack that job, no matter how highly motivated he was. Although he thought he was being humble by accepting the job, he was actually taking the first opportunity to end his very unpleasant job search.

Later, after sober reflection, he realized he didn't need a bundle of money to survive and start his climb back up—but he *did* have a very real *minimum acceptable starting wage.* He learned that by earning only $4.60 an hour and limiting his overtime to four hours on Saturday, he could bring home about $185 per week, and still have time and energy to pursue a permanent job search and attend his all-important AA meetings.

The counselor at the state Job Service will have a copy of the annual *Occupational Outlook*, published by the U. S. Department of Labor. (So does the Public Library.) This will supply a ballpark picture of what most occupations should pay. Your Prevailing Wage Office will bring the figure into sharper focus, and any Interviewer at the Job Service can tell you what the local job market is offering in a specific field.

You will take this information and add it to your compilation of minimum needs and come up with a minimum acceptable salary. This must be decided upon before you leave home for the company employment office. Then, if they can't meet this figure, you don't have to waste time agonizing over whether to try for it anyway. You have already decided, so you bust out of there and hustle up another interview.

Education

As with health and age questions, corporations are beginning to shy away from unwavering insistence on formal four-year degrees as a firm job prerequisite. If you read employment advertising carefully, you will note that employers are starting to talk around specific proof of graduation. Ads will specify "college preferred," "education in microbiology," "*should* have M.S. in engineering," or "degree or equivalent experience required."

It is much more important to beef up relevant education than to fill in line after line of innocuous credit courses. More education does not necessarily mean better. Nothing springs the trigger on the traditional personnel officer cop-out, which they call "over-qualified," like reading long lists of courses in Latin, Greek, teachings of Jesus, wisdom of the ages, art appreciation, and physical education.

The use of the crib sheet is an obvious must when dealing with the "Education" item on an application. Many forms will ask the number of semester hours you have in each college subject. Have these figured up in advance and grouped in categories. You should have a copy of your college transcript at hand; if not, order one immediately. In the meantime, reconstruct the hours from memory.

Rarely is one required to attach a college transcript to an application or present one to an interviewer. Exceptions are civil service jobs requiring a minimum number of hours in a given discipline, or positions in the field of education.

Retitle the courses to suit the job you are seeking, and lump irrelevant credits under umbrella categories. Our friend, E. Z. Duzzit, is still looking for a drafting job, but his two years at Community College were a little weak in this subject.

His transcript looked like this:

1st Semester		2nd Semester	
English Comp. I	3 hrs	English Comp. II	3 hrs
Swimming	2 hrs	Swimming	2 hrs
Art I	3 hrs	Art II	3 hrs
Algebra I	3 hrs	Algebra II	3 hrs
Spanish I	3 hrs	Spanish II	3 hrs
3rd Semester		4th Semester	
Business I	3 hrs	Business II	3 hrs
Plane Geometry	3 hrs	Solid Geometry	3 hrs
Mech. Drawing	3 hrs	Mechanical Drawing	3 hrs
Art Appreciation	2 hrs	Trigonometry	2 hrs
Sculpture	2 hrs	Sculpture	2 hrs

This was reduced to the following on his Crib Sheet and copied on all applications for drafting jobs:

Drafting, Mechanical Drawing, Industrial Arts, and
Related Subjects............................20 hours
Science..................................18 hours
Humanities................................16 hours

You will see that he put all his art courses into "Related Subjects," along with his primary selling group. He also rationalized trigonometry up to the top, giving that group more weight. Business was included as an industrial science. The balance of his courses were lumped together as "Humanities."

This type of arrangement required no explanations, was honest and could be backed up if necessary, and, more importantly, *was what the personnel people wanted to see.*

High School Education. So far we've been speaking primarily about a job seeker with some college or other further education. This is because employers rarely ask specifics about high school curriculum. We do want to make a very important point about holders of G.E.D, originally the General Educational Development test, but now more familiarly called the General Education

Diploma. Many applications that we have reviewed had a "no" checked next to the question of high school graduation, when farther down on the form——possibly in the section on military experience——there is mention of a G.E.D. If you have a G.E.D., you *have* a high school diploma. You have graduated. There is no need to qualify or modify this. If the question about high school graduation is asked, you should simply say "yes." Period.

High School References. By the way, high school teachers have excellent memories and are good writers. They are also sensitive people who are particularly gratified that a former student might consider them as a reference. If it hasn't been too many years since high school and you are a little short on relevant references, you will want to think about your mechanical arts or chemistry teacher when applying for that drafting or lab job. Of course, they should always be contacted first, their memories of you refreshed, and their references tested.

Work Experience

This item is really what this book is all about. If your work history were a beautiful chronology of successful employment, like Mr. Clean, you wouldn't be out of work. So, your occupational history must be worked out in detail, with all decisions made, and all backstopping planned, at *home*, before you start on your job-search rounds. The Crib Sheet should contain an absolute minimum of abbreviations on this subject.

It would naturally be more comfortable just to hand the receptionist a functional résumé, which smoothes over the gaps. But in real life, you will eventually have to fill out one of *their* forms, too, and this will ask you to list all jobs starting from the last and working backwards. It will want dates of employment, job descriptions, salaries, supervisors' names, and reasons for leaving.

Accounting for Gaps in Employment History. The recovering alcoholic job seeker is frequently overconcerned with gaps, as a heavy weight of guilt is associated with it. He is further intimidated if the application bears the browbeating admonition to "include all employment and account for any gaps in employment."

While the employment situation in the past eight years has been improving on the average, nationally, there have been many geographic zones of depressed employment and sporadic high unemployment in certain industries (e.g., oil and textiles). There have also been sudden mass layoffs of middle management due to mergers, foreign buy outs, and bankruptcies.

For these and many other reasons, personnel offices have become accustomed to seeing many applicants who have been "on the beach" for long periods. Six months or even over a year-and-a-half of job search has assumed normal status in management or specialized white-collar fields.

Many alcoholics, we realize, have extended this period beyond the eyebrow-raising point, and you may have concluded that a suitable cover story must be inserted. If this is what you have chosen to do—presuming you are aware of all of the perils and pitfalls of this choice of action—pay attention to the what other creative job applicants have learned.

Some cover stories were well thought out, both in justification and execution, and were successful. Some tried to "wing it" with humorous and tragic results. The cover stories that worked were the ones that were absolutely necessary, the dullest, the simplest, the most plausible, that were marginally true, and either easily backstopped or uncheckable.

For many reasons, which you should be aware of by now, many unemployed white-collar active-alcoholics go through periods of selling insurance and encyclopedias. While the disease rarely permits prolonged success in these fields, the alcoholic has no problem in initially selling himself as a salesman.

Recovered job seekers who have followed one or both routes don't hesitate to fill in the year or years they need on the application with the simple statement "Self-Employed; Licensed Insurance Broker," or "Self-Employed; Publications Broker." It doesn't matter if you were selling for Tibetan Casualty Insurance or the Encyclopedia of Erotica, commission salespersons are always self-employed. This precludes a possibly embarrassing and unnecessary reference check. Since you will have picked up enough of the trade jargon to schlepp through a bit of emergency conversation, you will have followed the traditional guidelines for cover stories: short, simple, dull, plausible, marginally true, and noncontradictable.

I have also seen this black hole of inactivity covered with the entry "assisted in family enterprise." It is always more comfortable if one *has* a family enterprise with which to associate this cover, but this is not necessary. An activity as personal as this would not be checked—relatives are not considered objective references.

One woman we worked with had used this story to cover a large gap in employment repeatedly as she attained progressively higher positions in her sober vocational recovery. Only once did an interviewer start to go into that area of her background. She cut him off with, "Certain members of my family pooled assets on an investment that was only marginally successful. I'm not at liberty to discuss it as the others are still speculating."

Besides simplicity, the key to any cover story is restriction of its use to absolute necessity. If you have decided to use one, you must follow this unalterable axiom: *a cover story must never be volunteered.* We hope this is a trait you left at the bar.

My personal favorite of all "cover stories" is the following, and I have never had a client get in trouble with it:

> *Fortunately, we had saved our money, so when I became unemployed I was able to conduct a careful search for the right position without pressure and panic.*

Employers interviewed after hire have told me they were impressed with the applicant's self-reliance, forward thinking, dependability, and candor.

THE FUNCTIONAL RESUME

Most new job seekers and career changers spend an inordinate amount of time, money, and aggravation on a résumé, and then use it the wrong way. The recovering alcoholic is particularly susceptible to misuse of the résumé because it permits him to kid friends, family, and himself into believing that he is really conducting a job search by mailing out hundreds of résumés.

A résumé is a product description of a job seeker written in a manner to appeal to the prospective employer. The personnel departments of employing corporations use these offerings as a mechanism for screening *out*——eliminating for further consideration——all but a few candidates. Just as in baseball or theater tryouts, the first cuts are not made by the team manager or the play director.

The "first readers" are lower level functionaries in the personnel department who are instructed to look for certain characteristics and experiences. But when swamped with résumés they will inevitably resort to very personalized and arbitrary methods for reducing the backlog. For instance, they may eliminate all single-spaced or multiple-paged offerings. Sloppy duplication or typos can insure a position in the first cut, as can great quantities of irrelevant detail. The latter problem is of particular concern to recovering alcoholics.

Since the recent years of most alcoholics have been considerably less than a career-building spectacle, there is a tendency to dwell on the halcyon days when drinking was a lifestyle and not a grave illness. A former intelligence officer friend could not bring himself to delete oriental languages and spy-related training from his résumé. This represented the last time in his life when he believed he had given his best; the last period his perfectionist personality would allow him to address with pride.

Alcoholics who have had marginal success at dozens of short-term, unrelated jobs will tend to list them all in great detail. We had one man tell us that trimming down his résumé was like trying to decide which of his children to throw out of an overcrowded lifeboat.

Usually, your résumé should be used only to supplement a letter to a company official requesting an interview. We have heard this letter called a "cover letter," "broadcast letter," and "introduction letter." I call it the *Ignition Letter*, and its only purpose is to start the interview engine. Any other use of the résumé or Ignition Letter is dishonest.

Many recovering job seekers have wasted much precious time dwelling on this traditional fantasy: A company president is working late some night, going over a batch of résumé s, when he comes across yours. "Eureka! This is just the person we need to take over the new Office of Incidental Advisories we've been thinking about setting up." He picks up the phone and gives you a call. You're out, but he talks to your wife. When you come home, she throws her arms around you and tells you the news. "Darlin', the young'uns and I are *so* proud of you!" Curtain. Applause.

Only a dummy buys a pig in a poke, and corporate officers don't get there by being dummies. We will discuss the Ignition Letter in detail later in this chapter. The résumé is to be used only as an appendix to this letter. And the Ignition Letter *and* résumé have but one purpose——*to get an interview.*

Your Job Service and the public library will have résumé guides, along with excellent books on job search that include tips on the preparation of a résumé . I suggest you look these over, remembering that they are designed for Mr. or Ms. Clean. The most popular résumé is one that closely resembles an application form. After the introductory personal description and educational summary, there appears a chronological listing of work experience. This obviously does *not* suit the purposes of most alcoholics.

I suggest that my imperfect readers consider the Functional Résumé for their personal advertising campaigns. The application form is an attempt to squeeze the square-pegged alcoholic into a round-holed Ms. or Mr. Clean. Why should you copy this cruel mechanism when composing the one document over which you have absolute control? *Remember: The application is the employer's weapon. The Functional Résumé is the job seeker's weapon.* Its only purpose is to get you an interview!

In preparing the Functional Résumé , you will go through the following five steps:

1. You write a brutally honest chronological résumé , omitting nothing——good or bad. Most recovering alcoholics retain a hangup of guilt that makes it easier to write a confessional of heinous failures than to remember little islands of success

in that wasteland. A trick that sometimes works is to write the first draft in the third person. Corny and crude entries are acceptable if they are totally honest.

He worked his way up in three months from laborer to assistant foreman in a plastics factory with absolutely no knowledge of the process or industry. Everybody liked him, and wanted to work on his shift. He was offered a management trainee job. He saved the company much money by spotting a major error. He made corrections in safety procedures that may have prevented injuries and damage suits. He started taking more sick days, finally forgetting to call in. After a week of absence without leave, he stopped in, picked up his check, and quit in anticipation of being fired.

This is going to require some time and thought. Your family can possibly help with this, as you undoubtedly mentioned little glory moments to them at the time they occurred.

2. Make a topical list of major functions that would be important considerations for a recruiter in a target company. An applicant for a position with an engineering firm would possibly list some of the following functions:

> Research and Design
> Sales Engineering
> Scientific and Technical Coordination
> Industrial Engineering Technical Work
> Technical Writing
> Management and Supervision

If your goal is in the merchandising field, you might list such functions as:

> Sales
> Service
> Purchasing
> Demonstration

> Contract Negotiation
> Sales Engineering
> Promotion and Publicity
> Promotional and Technical Writing
> Management and Supervision

3. Next, you take each function you've listed in order, and go back to your mercilessly honest work history, lifting anything remotely relating to that function from every job you ever had. *This also should include volunteer work or other unpaid activities.*

We know a recovering alcoholic who was seeking work in personnel service. His Functional Résumé included, under the topic "Industrial Relations," mention of participation in a weekly seminar consisting of doctors, psychiatrists, social workers, and personnel specialists on the subject of industrial alcoholism. This was quite true. He didn't mention, however, that the seminars took place in the psychiatric ward of the Veterans Hospital where he was a patient and that this was part of his prescribed group therapy.

You will now have many worthy accomplishments listed under each function. Forget that they came from different jobs and avocations over a long period.

4. List several prominent firms or institutions that would be respected by a prospective employer and where you have trustworthy contacts (you've checked them out, of course!). They will be listed at the bottom of the résumé, almost as if by afterthought, i.e., "Responsible individuals in General Electric, Southern Bell, and RCA who have knowledge of my qualifications are prepared to provide references if required."

These need not be restricted to former employers! You may not have worked for any of these companies; they may have been customers of yours when you were selling tools for Hicktown Hardware. Customers usually do not have a good idea of vendors' personal problems and sales records; they are usually exposed to only the best side of sales people.

5. The final step is to eliminate everything that doesn't fit snugly into the selected functions, limiting each accomplishment to a sentence or paring a couple into a single phrase. You are listing functions, not an employment history.

Here is an excerpt from a Functional Résumé used successfully by a recovering alcoholic in the engineering field:

MANAGEMENT AND SUPERVISION

Received commendation for operational and administrative supervision of forty skilled electronics and mechanical technicians working on highly classified, multi-million dollar government project.

The well-organized mind of the personnel officer who scanned the résumé and screened him "in" for an interview probably presumed this had reference to employment with a giant, such as GE or Rockwell, which he had mentioned at the bottom of the page. GE and Rockwell, of course, were only customers of his during his shaky selling career with Hicktown Hardware.

The skilled technicians he supervised were Air Force Mechanics and the highly classified project was a B-52 bomber our ex-sergeant and his crew maintained.

Women who enter the job market after years of devotion to homemaker duties will find this functional style particularly useful. Of course, they will eventually have to explain that the "direct sales for a major national corporation" was door-to-door Girl Scout Cookie peddling, and that "management and supervision" involved the very real responsibility of running a household and directing the lives of teenagers. This can be interpreted with logical humor at the face-to-face interview——the only goal of a résumé.

THE IGNITION LETTER

The purpose of the Ignition Letter is to start the engine running that will lead to an employment interview. The Ignition Letter is simply a personal letter to a *particular* person asking for an appointment to discuss a matter of importance to both of you. It is not a "To Whom It May Concern" cover letter slapped on top of a résumé and mailed to "Personnel Office, Acme Bubble Gum Company."

There are thousands of unemployed "Mr. Clean" types pounding the pavement and sending in résumé s. You have obstacles that they don't have, and you must increase the odds in your favor.

I'll give a few examples of Ignition Letters, but it will be impossible to design a model and retain its intimacy. You may or may not decide to attach a résumé ; generally, I advise against it. If you show too many hole cards before the interview, that excess information will be used to screen you *out*. Unless you run into a situation where the job description looks as if it were designed around your résumé , it's best to avoid showing it until the last moment. Even then, the reader will always know much more about the job as he or she sees it than does any applicant.

I was once involved in a research project centering on a group of veterans who were referred to various large companies in the area. All were well-qualified for the open positions and should have been competitive. The question being investigated was: Why were some eliminated before an interview, others after the interview, and the successful candidates ultimately chosen? In many instances of early elimination, our *post-mortem* study revealed that the résumé had reared its ugly head.

One veteran vying for an opening in the market analysis section of a mail order company had heavy experience in exactly that type of work on the West Coast. Although this was accurately described in his résumé , there was also an innocent mention that his college major was French and the fact that he had taught the language for a year as a civilian and for six months in the army.

We recorded the following statement from the personnel specialist who was responsible for putting his application in the "no interview" pile. "He couldn't use that French on this job. Why, all the people up in that department are Italians——well, maybe a couple of Jews."

Of course, there are many positions for which an advance résumé is a firm prerequisite for an interview. Even in these cases, we have seen best results when an Ignition Letter is first sent to a particular *named* officer of the company, and a résumé requested by him.

Is there any difference in the handling of a query or complaint directed to a high official of an organization and one coming up through the regular channels? Those of us who have spent years in middle management will automatically reply, "Absolutely none at all!" Wouldn't we love to believe that were actually the case?

Regardless of our good intentions and any idealistic office policy, *anything that comes down from a higher echelon receives different treatment than the same thing coming up from the street.* And the odds that the different treatment also will be better treatment are overwhelming. On this obstacle course, the winners always play the odds. Letters to the President or to a member of Congress *always* find their way to an appropriate desk on the "front line," and they are *always* answered promptly and courteously.

Years ago when I worked in vocational counseling with a state employment service, we used to keep a folder on "Congressional Inquiries" and "White House Mail." A postcard to the President of the United States in a drunken scrawl generated an extraordinary call-in, an hour of counseling, special job search efforts, and other individual attention until the postcard writer——with whose wine time we were interfering——begged us to stop. All this exceptional treatment was then dutifully reported up the line to the White House Mail Office.

No positive step taken in a job search is a waste of time if one is not kidding oneself and follows the other rules of the game. Even flat rejections give the experience and practice in Ignition Letter-writing and telephone follow-up that will hone the blade for future assaults on the job market. If, for example, an Ignition Letter is addressed to Simeon Stonewall, President of Uppity Frocks, and the following terse reply is received:

> *Mr. Stonewall does not accept solicitations for employment with Uppity Company. Please direct your queries to our Personnel Department.*
>
>   *Robert Bootlick*
>   *Asst. to the President*

Wow! A personal invitation from the Assistant to the President of Uppity Frocks to make an application for employment. We now find the name of the manager of the Personnel Department and dash off the following Ignition Letter:

> *Dear Mr. Grindstone,*
>   *Bob Bootlick from Simeon Stonewall's office has asked that I contact you to discuss the opening in the Strapless Gown Department . . . .*

This approach is almost always effective with larger companies, but with midsized firms, you probably will want to make your move with the employment office by telephone. This will give you the opportunity to get an interview appointment before they have time to check it out through channels.

> *Hello, Manny Grindstone? E. Z. Duzzit here, formerly with Gullible Garments. I just got a note from Bob Bootlick . . . you know, in Mr. Stonewall's office? He suggested I get in touch with you regarding an opening in the Strapless Gown Department. I'd like to make it today, if possible . . .*

Your Ignition Letters will be personalized, if possible, but will never be cute or flip: You are writing to a serious businessperson. It will be short: You are writing to a busy businessperson. It will show knowledge of the organization or product: You are writing to a proud businessperson. It will show that person, in a few sentences, how you can help the company make more money. Because you are *not* writing to a *stupid* businessperson.

Dear Ms. Boss,
   I was happy to hear of your plans to establish a branch of your Flange Division in our city. While my experience in this field has been as a maintenance engineer with your competition, I have always respected your quality product.
   I have some ideas that I believe will make your transition to this area easier and your local operation more profitable. I would like to discuss them with you or your representative at the earliest opportunity . . .

***

Dear Ms. Uppancoming,
   I have followed your career in Gussett Industries, and was pleased, but not surprised, to learn that you were selected to head the Western division. I share your philosophy of 'zero defects' in production, and have some ideas I would like to discuss with you. I believe I can be of particular assistance to your Fission Division in the elimination of rejected boomers . . .

Because of the personal nature of Ignition Letters, I'm not going to cite a volume of examples. Just remember that they should show product familiarity, ideas for profit increase or cost cutting, and try to weave in a personal connector with the addressee if possible. This also helps when the letter is bucked downstairs with a simple "Handle This" slip attached. The "buckee" usually doesn't know just how to "handle this" when the letter is from a brother or sister in the boss's lodge, fraternity, sorority, or branch of the military service.

A former client, who had tried unsuccessfully to get past the receptionist at the interview desk at a particularly popular company, took our advice and did an end run with a letter to the owner. He didn't mention his other attempts at employment, but very briefly outlined his background for the job——a blue-collar production position.

In the final paragraph, standing alone, he added, "Like yourself, I am a former marine, so you know exactly what I mean when I offer you competent, dependable, and loyal service."

Although the personnel manager of this company had told us often before that "Absolutely Never!" would he be influenced by an end run or implied pressure from upstairs, our man suddenly was called in for an interview and was working within a week.

Even on short holes, professional golfers do not aim for the pin from the tee. The purpose of the initial drive and approach shots is for position—to get on the green. The approach shots you have made so far are to get in good position for an attack on the flag. A successful drive is one that gives the player a good lie on the fairway from which the green can be reached. Successful efforts at target research, crib preparation, and Ignition Letters are the ones that produce *interviews*.

6

TARGET RESEARCH

The *selection of targets by an alcoholic job seeker requires strict discipline*. You must exercise a high degree of moderation, restraint, and control in your selection of the potential employers, or "targets," you intend to confront seriously. Remember, alcoholics are perfectionists with inferiority complexes. They will normally follow the path of least resistance, allowing themselves to believe they are doing something worthwhile, while presenting the least threat of embarrassing rejection.

There is a theory you will see expounded in many books on job search called the "numbers game." According to this technique, a hundred résumés sent out will produce five interviews. The numbers vary from book to book, but it doesn't matter, as they are equally false. Saturation bombing based on poor intelligence wiped out many quiet suburbs, forests, and rice paddies in recent wars, while a single flight zeroed in on a well-identified and located target would produce a much greater military advantage. Ten thousand résumés scattered to the winds become very expensive confetti extruded from mindless shredders.

A couple of years ago I was invited to an office party given by the personnel department of a major corporation. As the chiefs and Indians toasted the New Year and began looking and acting foolish, we were interrupted by something that sounded like a freight train roaring through the next office. The manager noted my concern, and explained over his eggnog that they were merely cleaning out the files. This office received hundreds of unsolicited résumé s each year, and only a few were selected by the "first readers" as of potential interest to the selection unit. The rest were stored in cabinets and boxes in a far corner of the personnel suite.

The annual office party, held between Christmas and New Year's Day, was considered "down time," and so was chosen for the traditional ritual of feeding these rejects into the shredder. I wandered into the next room to greet the team of volunteers who had developed a rhythmically efficient method of removing staples, separating the thicker résumé s, inserting appropriate numbers of pages into the screeching shredder, and sipping their bourbon-laced cups of cheer without missing a beat.

Each neatly typed offering lifted from a box represented the hopes and dreams of someone——a real person out there. The monster screamed, and out came bag after bag of multicolored packing material. I wondered how many of those people were still out of work; still sitting by the phone or mailbox thinking that their résumé s were in there working for them. Please spare yourself this depressing experience. The time you spend clearly defining and identifying targets will save time, money, and heartbreak.

By now, I pray you have gotten rid of the totally dishonest hair shirt of "I'm so desperate I'll go anywhere and do anything for any amount of money." "Doing anything" is false humility.

The recovering alcoholic is a demon for work, and having more stamina than most of his co-workers, will have the capacity to learn almost any new job. But the perfectionist alcoholic cannot stand to turn in a poor or even average performance for more than a minimum break-in period.

If you have been an office worker all of your life, and have little mechanical aptitude or experience, the frustrations you may experience attempting to excel at a "hands-on" occupation may jeopardize your sobriety. We've often heard recovering addicts with white collar backgrounds say, "I'll do anything; I'll even dig ditches." Have you ever tried to dig ditches for a living? I have. I got fired.

Here you can call upon your aptitude test results (The GATB, covered in chapter 2. Changing a field of work upon achieving sobriety can be an exciting and rewarding step in recovery, but you must be warned not to expect sobriety to *change* your talents and aptitudes. Decisions come hard for sober alcoholics; they were very easy when alcohol was used to lubricate the process. As a recovering alcoholic or addict, you must never confuse the impulsive acts of drinking days with real, sober, grown-up decisions. You must decide now——in broad terms but with definite boundaries——where you are going to work, what type of work you are going to do, and the minimum wage you can accept.

HEADQUARTERS: THE LIBRARY

I have always recommended that the public library——this free facility——become a job seeker's headquarters. You have already decided where to look for work first, and generally what kinds of jobs you want to take a shot at. You are going to shoot for an absolute minimum of one interview a day and an average of two.

The librarian can direct you to the Business Reference Section. You should go directly to the librarian and ask questions and directions immediately upon arrival instead of doing the alcoholic thing——wandering around for an hour hoping to come across what you're looking for.

This may seem like a trifle, but this phoney pride and pseudo self-sufficiency is really a mask for the alcoholic inferiority complex. I've known recovering alcoholics to waste an entire morning looking for a factory or office building rather than ask directions. Furthermore, every sober exchange you have with a stranger helps prepare you for a smooth, unruffled interview. Here are a few samples of the library tools you will find useful:

State Industrial Directory

Most libraries also will have directories of neighboring states. This reference will have all industrial firms arranged by geographic location and by product category. It will have the address, the phone number, size—both in square feet and employment population (the latter broken down by male, female, management, and production). There also will be listed names and titles of the major officers and a description of the product or service.

These books usually come out annually, and their accuracy and usefulness will vary from state to state. I have seen some quite professional directories and some that are sloppy efforts, so outdated that I suspected their revisions consisted solely of changing the date on the cover. Never depend on a single source of information.

Standard & Poor's Directory of Corporate Officers and Executives

This volume is regularly updated with paperback supplements and will be extremely valuable, provided the target company is a major corporation or a subsidiary of a biggie.

Moody's Handbook of Common Stocks

Again, for the big ones. If you are targeting a corporation listed in this reference, you will find intimate information on the company's business, past performances, plans, and prognosis. Besides helpful decision input, this information can load you with intimate ammunition for your job interview.

Special Directories

These include volumes on selected industries; their usefulness would be a matter of happy chance. Examples are *Modern Plastics Encyclopedia* and *Metal Finishing Guidebook and Directory*.

Business and Industry Periodicals

Depending upon the size and arrangement of your library, these magazines may be in the business department or incorporated with other magazines and periodicals. Until you wander through the trade magazine section of a large library, you will have no idea of the scope of this industry. There are well-illustrated, professionally written, and informative periodicals specifically published for every conceivable industry or service.

Vocational Counselors, Mortuary Suppliers, Prison Administrators, Fire Extinguisher Manufacturers, Concrete Companies, Restaurant and Bar Suppliers, and even former spies have their own magazines. There is even a trade magazine for people who publish trade magazines!

To keep up with the current buzz words and to ensure currency in a field from which you may have been absent for months or years, you will want to check these trade journals for one applicable to your situation. You may be surprised to find a magazine devoted specifically to your specialty. Frequently these trade journals are sent to members of a trade or professional association and end up only in the desks or living rooms of front office executives. Sometimes you will find a classified section in the back of one of these magazines with "Help Wanted" listings, but more often these are used for "Situation Wanted" insertions.

Thomas Register

We have rarely found a library—large, small, big city or home town—that did not have this basic tool of industry in its reference collection. It might not be this year's edition, but it will be there. The *Thomas Register* consists of twelve hefty volumes, each about the size of a Manhattan phone book. Volumes I through VII list products by the modified noun system; such as "Nuts, Galvanized." There follows, by state and city, listings of manufacturers or suppliers of that product, with addresses. There is also a symbol representing the estimated volume of business in the most recent reporting period—AAAA means $1 million plus; AAA is over

$500 thousand, etc. down to D (over $10 thousand) and X (not enough information on which to base an estimate).

Volume VII also includes a product index with over 100,000 trade names. Volume VIII lists over 95,000 companies by state, and gives information on company officers, warehouses, distributors, sales offices, subsidiaries, and affiliated and controlled companies. Volumes IX through XII contain catalogues of many companies listed in previous volumes. Although this is an abridged reference, if you are lucky and your target company's catalogue is included, you have a real bonus.

Major Newspapers

Your library will have a collection of papers from the state capital and the largest cities in your area, besides local papers. The Sunday employment sections should be carefully scanned—not only the "Help Wanted" classified ads, but the section devoted to advertisements for professional, technical, sales, and managerial openings in prominent companies.

At this point there should be no concern with the type of opening a particular company may have. You are spotting firms with *hiring activity*. If they are in need of engineers, they will require technicians and operators later. Major hiring in production departments usually generates openings in personnel, fiscal, and other administrative departments.

Daily Newspaper Scan. The daily and Sunday "Help Wanted" classifieds will, of course, be routinely checked. This is because you have trained yourself to use every device that's free. After the first three or four days, this scan should never take more than ten minutes, because, you will have learned the following:

Recognize the repeaters, or permanent ads. They remind us of a factory in Newark, New Jersey, that was notorious in employment circles for having atrocious working conditions and an understandably high turnover. Under the firm's name, directly on the side of the building in large block letters, was painted "HELP WANTED."

Recognize and Eliminate "Agency" Ads. These will be appealing ads, general in nature, quoting seductive salaries and fringe benefits, and no company name. The ad will direct you to send a résumé to a box number at the newspaper, or to call a certain number and ask for "Mr. Shifty." Ads placed by commercial employment agencies are usually the "composite ads" we discussed in a previous chapter. When confronted with these little deceptions, the agencies will reply that the ads "represent a sample of the type of positions regularly available through our service." The actual purpose, of course, is to build up a large reservoir of applicants that can be screened for salable bodies. Ethical private agencies are excellent avenues for job search if you have highly marketable skills and experience, and you can afford the service. On the other hand, ethical private agencies rarely run composite ads.

Recognize "blind ads"——those without names of a firm, only a box number. These may be composite ads, but are also frequently used by companies for very legitimate reasons. Internally, an announcement of an opening could immediately start ominous rumors of an ax about to fall on incumbent bookkeepers. Some might even defect to another firm in paranoid anticipation. Another reason for the blind ad is industrial intelligence. News of personnel activity in a particular department can be valuable to a rival company, a bargaining customer, or an avaricious conglomerate bent on hostile takeover.

But the most common use of the blind ad——and the most important for our purposes——is to allow the employer's personnel people to screen *out* candidates at their leisure, without having to deal with all those bothersome personal interviews. Your motivation is different, in that you are *looking* for interviews. You don't have time for any employment process that is set up to eliminate you from that interview. Neither can you afford the postage and printing costs of mailing résumés to every blind ad that appears in the paper.

There are several ways of dealing with a blind ad. Some of our friends have rented their own P.O. Box and sent in blind responses. We prefer a post card reply such as this:

"Gentlemen: My experience and achievements amply qualify me for the announced opening. I can assure you I am not one of your present employees, and will be happy to provide a résumé and arrange for an interview upon identification of your company. Sincerely, E. Z. Duzzit (with address and phone).

If you get no response, you're only out the price of a postcard and you have eliminated a time-wasting encounter with an agency or itinerant encyclopedia peddler. Any positive identifications that you receive by phone or mail will then be placed on your spotting list for the "vetting" cycle. You will, of course, respond immediately to any overt advertisement that announces an opening suitable to your ability and requirements, and that apparently has potential.

Check the Business Section. Scan the paper for all items referring to plant expansion, awarding of new contracts, moving of companies into your area, and promotion or appointments of executives. This information will be noted in detail and retained for use in your Ignition Letter.

By now you have accumulated a long spotting list of target companies. You have gotten the names from personal knowledge of famous local firms, friends' recommendations, the newspapers, the *State Industrial Directory*, the Yellow Pages of the phone book, and the *Thomas Register*. And you've added to this list suggestions from the Job Service interviewer or counselor.

VETTING

We have borrowed this noble term from British intelligence; it refers to expert examination and appraisal of information, individuals, or groups. You will have found as much information as possible—within a realistic period—on each target. Now you have the facts necessary to make an intelligent judgment to keep a target on your list or drop it, and to set your priorities.

At this point we start a new list, writing in the information you've found about a target company after its name. The order of the information isn't important if you keep it consistent. This helps to spot blank spaces in the intelligence-gathering process, and makes it easier for you to compare companies when setting priorities. You should now be able to compile the following minimum dossier for each target company on your "shopping list."

- Exact location, checked on city map; phone number.
- How to get there and back (by public transportation, if possible—include bus routes and schedules).
- Employment population of the company, broken down by male, female, production, office, and sales.
- Corporate lineage - who *really* owns the company?
- Capitalization and production or sales figures.
- Company product descriptions (*definitely check this out!*).
- Company officers' important biographical points will have been noted from *Standard & Poor's, Who's Who in American Business,* or local Chamber of Commerce Directories. Executives write their *own* biographical sketches for these publications; therefore, any listed affiliation or accomplishment is something of which they are proud. A note can be made of things in common— such as birthplace, college, fraternity or sorority, branch of military service, favorite sport or charity, and so forth.
- Intelligence garnered from trade magazines or business sections of newspapers regarding each firm's activities. With larger companies, the *Reader's Guide* for the past year will be checked to see if they have been the subject of magazine articles.

Of course the detail of compliance with the above suggestions will depend on the level of job you are seeking and the size, nature, and complexity of the target company. But I warn you, the skimping you do on this exercise is inversely proportionate to the degree of success in attaining permanent employment with advancement potential. In other words, you get out of the exercise what you put into it.

SELECTION

You have now dropped from your list all companies that you know in your heart you would not work for. Before any name is eliminated, however, meditate a bit on the honesty of your selection process. Are you dropping a target company from consideration because you have learned that their product or service is far afield from your experience, or that they are on mass lay-off and on the verge of bankruptcy? Or, are they being eliminated because you are afraid they won't hire you? These companies have highly paid, full-time personnel people whose job it is to reject applicants. Make them earn their money! Don't try to do their job for them.

Priority rating should now begin. Group the first batch of ten target companies according to location around two "dream boat" companies. A "dream boat" is a firm you would be working for if your skills were in high demand and you had an unblemished record. Don't let yourself spend too much time on priorities, as you will eventually cover the entire list. When we use the word "priority" we refer only to order of contact.

You are going to get better and better at writing Ignition Letters, and will become more skillful, organized, and relaxed in your job interviews. As skill and confidence increase, you will start enjoying this once frightening and painful experience. This is because addictive people are perfectionists, and they enjoy the recognition that they are getting good at something. This includes the mystique of job search, and fear begins to turn into pleasant excitement.

So, you see, you will not want to put all of your "dream boats" in your first batch of contacts. You are building skills, and one of the beauties of a sober job search is that you will very shortly be in a position rejecting job offers. This is a luxury you haven't honestly enjoyed for years.

CIVIL SERVICE JOBS

Exploring civil service possibilities should be an early task of the recovering alcoholic job seeker. Most people's understanding of state and federal civil service is limited to the few functionaries that we deal with personally when doing business with the government. The Unemployment Office, Auto License Bureau, and tax people round out the lot. Many of you will be able to add law enforcement officers, judges, and probation officers to this list.

Actually, there are parallel jobs in government for every job in the private sector. There are government truck drivers, accountants, pharmacists, barbers, drafters, landscapers, electricians, plumbers, civilian pilots, musicians, conservationists, civilian sailors, health technicians, computer programmers, lab technicians, carpenters, travel agents, artists, chefs, golf pros, teachers in overseas American schools, store managers, fire fighters, substance abuse counselors, and hundreds of thousands of administrators.

Instead of considering government work as a last resort, the recovering alcoholic should consider it first. In the first place it takes a long, long time to progress from civil service application filing, through selections for consideration, interview, final selection, and actual employment. The play is to file several applications, then treat them like lottery tickets——forget them and continue with the job search. If one comes through, it will be a pleasant diversion in the routine and might become a windfall career.

The Civil Service has many advantages that the alcoholic should consider apart from the obvious fringe benefits and other security prerequisites. First, the government cannot, by law, discriminate because of age or alcoholism history (except in certain law enforcement and intelligence categories). Secondly, the pace and regular hours usually encountered will be unlikely to jeopardize a recovering substance abuser's sobriety, while a hectic, competitive position in private business might.

A mistake most people make when targeting a civil service job as a second career is that they aim too high. Don't let the modest salaries of lower government jobs fool you. The fringe benefits are great and there is ample room at the top. The recovering alcoholic who is assiduously working at his sobriety has an almost unfair advantage over the nonalcoholic in government work, and promotions come with surprising regularity. The alcoholic personality seems to adapt to the spurts and lulls of government work.

But the impatient alcoholic who aims at senior-level positions as a starting point in his new governmental career, whatever his educational or practical qualifications, should be prepared for a disappointing wait of several years——or eternity. While many announcements are open to all applicants (many are limited to people already in civil service), the realities are that justice is blind only on statues in front of the court house.

A board will certify a group of apparently qualified applicants, basing their opinions on a study of the application forms. A senior person from the department that has the opening——one with an intimate knowledge of the job (probably the person who will supervise the announced job) will then interview the certified applicant.

It makes sense that most management people with wide knowledge of the field——and the senior people in that field——will have someone in mind when they are empowered to fill a senior vacancy. These jobs are usually rigged to be filled by promotion from within or by transfer. If, for some rare reason, this is impossible, each opening will have a highly competitive pool of thousands of applicants.

State civil service openings are relatively easy to find, most states issuing periodic bulletins with details of openings and specifications. These can be obtained by visiting or writing the state civil service office in the capital or a major city in your state. Federal job openings are not that visible. All state capitals and major cities used to have Federal Employment Information Centers; however, many of these have been cut by budgetary restrictions. Those still functioning will be listed in your phone directory under U. S. Government, possibly under Office of Personnel Management (OPM). If you have access to such a Center in your area, check it out.

Every fifteen days, on the first and fifteenth of each month, the OPM will publish a listing of all Federal job openings in your state, or surrounding area. *It is important for you to get on the permanent mailing list for these bulletins!* They will show the job title, location, starting salary and possible advancements, experience and educational requirements, and if a written test is required. And——pay attention to this——it will give a *closing date*. If you are remotely interested in an opening, you should send a postcard to the address given, list the announcement date, and get it postmarked before the closing date. The office with the opening will then send a package with additional information and a blank SF 171 form for filing.

This biweekly bulletin will not list *all* openings in government. Some job openings are only circulated inside the departments holding the openings. There are several reasons for this. Some job openings are limited to people with "status"; who are already in federal civil service. Others are further restricted to applicants who are currently working in the very department having the opening. It is also a sad truism that some jobs are "wired." In other words, the hiring agency already has someone in mind for the position, and is going through the ritual of "announcing" the opening just to comply with the formalities of the Civil Service Law.

If you have any friends or relatives in government, it is important to ask them to query their personnel offices for current announcements regularly. It is the usual practice for the central personnel office in Washington to send *all* announcements to branch offices all over the country. Since few people in field stations are looking for jobs, these are routinely circulated to the local staff with other junk mail and then discarded. Personnel offices of many governmental departments will put you on their mailing list by request.

Some of you will be willing——or may actually want——to relocate to another region. Be aware that this is a frequent impulse in not-quite-sober alcoholics trying to effect a "geographic cure" of their addiction. In practical terms, you probably will experience an added problem in being selected for interview for a job in a remote location.

In the federal picture, the successful candidate will usually live within commuting range of the job site, no matter how eloquently a willingness to relocate is proclaimed. People charged with the job of interview and selection know that many are called but few are chosen. They hesitate to ask an applicant to travel from Peoria to Denver for an interview when the possibility of their prevailing over all other candidates is slim. When I have a counselee who has a healthy interest in relocation *and* has the financial resources plus the necessary physical and emotional stamina to travel frequently on unsuccessful interview jaunts, I advise him or her to insert a sentence similar to this in the cover letter:

> *For personal family reasons I have decided to relocate in Denver (or Dallas or wherever), and anticipate accomplishing this move within the next six months.*

Do not elaborate on this. There is no need for a cover story or fabrication here. The purpose is to get an interview, and once this is accomplished, it doesn't matter what the personal family reasons are.

When some department or agency of the federal government is in a mass hiring mode, entry level career positions are filled through a general examination. This has most recently been called PACE, for Professional and Administrative Career Examination. It covered entry level positions with annual salaries of up to the vicinity of $20 thousand. Now, the government is going through one of its cyclical "freeze" modes. Technically, this means that there is little hiring, and even if someone dies or retires, the position may not be filled. Do not be intimidated by rumors or reports that there is a freeze on federal hiring.

Freezes come and freezes go, but the federal government keeps right on hiring. *You should visit the nearest Office of Personnel Management (OPM) in your area.* Call for an appointment (in the blue pages of your phone book under U.S. Government, Office of Personnel Management), and get the current picture on recruitment in your area. When they know you are not looking for a specific job on a specific timetable, they will *love* to have you come down and talk. Government people are always tickled pink to talk in nonthreatening generalities. The representative you talk with may say, "There is a permanent freeze on hiring," which, of course, technically would mean he or she is out of a job. Other answers we've heard are, "We're only taking applications from college graduates," or "The only positions we're testing for now are clerical." This may very well change with the next mail delivery or phone call to that office.

The US Postal Service announces its entry level examinations separately. This should be checked out directly with the post office, and a test preparation booklet located and borrowed at the library. There are several sample test booklets, but the most helpful and generally available are the ARCO publications. They are solid packed with sample tests that are very close to the real thing. They also contain very helpful guides to government employment test-taking.

Please don't be too concerned about the entry level pay scale. This is probably more money that you've made for some time, and the fringe benefits for you and your family, coupled with job security and incomparable upward mobility, make it a worthy *part* of your job search.

We have found that most alcoholics who are former government employees *quit* their good civil service jobs because of their alcoholism; very few were fired because of their alcoholism. We have worked with many of these folks in the initial stages of their recovery who refused to consider returning to any position lower than the one they left. When they finally got over that phony prideful hangover, they worried about the money. They remembered that they could barely make do with their salary when they resigned their high grade.

If this applies to you, I suggest you may have forgotten the fact that the reason you couldn't "make do" was that most of your pay went for booze or drugs. Furthermore, if you should take a lower paying job and dig in your sober heels, giving it your level best, accepting supervision, and soaking up knowledge with ambitious humility, you *will* get promoted—early and often. When advanced positions open, they *must* give first opportunities to in-house applicants. Clerk typists (now called word processor operators) usually start at GS-3 or GS-4. The GS-5 and GS-7 entry-level job openings are frequently classified as career ladder positions. In other words, a successful applicant can be promoted to a higher grade without further examination or competitive bidding. These grades are the windows to professional status in the bureaucracy, and you will find that most people who retire at high salaries with pompous titles started at one of these grades. In 1991, GS-5s started at $16,973 and GS-7s at $21,023. A four percent increase is expected as of January 1, 1992. You should request a current pay schedule from OPM along with up-to-date SF-171 forms, as government salaries are subject to annual cost-of-living increases.

If you are considering civil or postal service, you have probably come across advertisements from tabloid newspapers or match-book covers touting cram courses to prepare applicants for these jobs, or claiming to have an inside track on openings. Do not invest a nickel in these "schools" or "services." They are rip-offs!

For legitimate assistance, check your Public Library for the *Federal Times*. The *Federal Times* is a newspaper/magazine specializing in civil service news and views. This publication lists most current openings with accurate job descriptions and addresses for application. A careful reading of the announcement and a thorough study of available ARCO guides will prepare you quite well.

Several months after you file for an announced opening, you may receive a notice that you have been certified as eligible for the position. *This is not a job offer unless it specifically says so!* Half-a-year may have passed and all you have to show for your application is a piece of paper saying you are worthy. Not even an interview yet! Do you now see why it is recommended that you start this process early and, meanwhile, continue with your regular job search?

Before filling out the Standard Form 171 to apply for a government job, here is a tip that will improve your odds tremendously. (This advice is equally applicable to state and local job applications.) Carefully read the job description in the announcement and underline or **highlight** adjectives and verbs. For instance, if the announcement reads:

The incumbent will demonstrate a history of sedulous acumen in the performance of managerial administrative functions.

The wise applicant has highlighted **sedulous, acumen, performance, managerial, administrative, and demonstrate.** He'll then work into an appropriate spot in his SF 171 the following statement:

> *I have been commended for sedulous acumen in the performance of managerial administrative functions.*

This example is, of course, an exaggeration, but only a slight one. The first reader of your application will be a Personnel Classification Specialist. Her job is to match up the job description on the announcement with the qualifications of the applicant. She is a very powerful person. Unless she certifies an applicant as eligible, he won't even get to talk to the hiring department on the phone. Commonly she won't know beans about the job in question besides the announcement and a supplementary description available to her in the *Dictionary of Occupational Titles.* But she'll know how to read, and she'll know how to play the "Match Game."

If the announcement talks about "word processing," make sure you talk about "word processing," not just typing. If a health service announcement on AIDS research refers to it as "HIV Investigative Analysis," then that's the term the successful applicant should use. If the announcement asks about experience related to "information processing in a network environment," and you reply that you, "utilized modem linkage to remote mainframes," the department head that makes the final decision may be delighted with the answer. Unfortunately, the department head will never hear of you, because the first reader will not have recognized your qualifications as matching the announcement.

Pick up some copies of the SF 171 at a Federal Building, or write to the Office of Personnel Management: 1900 E Street NW, Washington, DC 20415. These forms are subject to occasional minor revision. The remarks below refer to SF 171 (Rev. 6-88). You can duplicate these as needed, but you should always have a few on hand for future filing. The instructions must be followed carefully, and the application must be filed before the closing date of the announcement. The first reader may not know much about the job opening, but she'll be razor sharp when it comes to dates.

Carefully consider the item pertaining to the lowest grade you will accept. A GS-5 or GS-7 is a modest but perfectly acceptable grade to request and will offer a better chance of early consideration than if GS-11 is inserted. Many job seekers make the mistake of putting in a higher figure, thinking they will negotiate down as necessary. It doesn't work that way! If the opening is for a GS-7 and the application states lowest salary acceptable is GS-8, the first reader will refer it to the shredder.

However, if you humbly insert GS-5 in that slot, make sure you note in Item 13 that you will only accept appointment locally or in a nearby city unless you are unburdened with dependents or still have ample savings to draw on. The federal government will pay moving expenses for the transfer of its people, but *not* for initial assignment.

A serious job seeker will have several *perfect* copies of an SF 171 on hand, with the first thirteen items left blank, to file for every opening of interest as it comes up.

The following items should be obvious to you by now, but go over them step by step, as people frequently get additionally intimidated when filling out government forms.

Item 19: Military Service. "Were you discharged from the military service under honorable conditions?" (If your discharge was changed to 'honorable' or 'general' by a Discharge Review Board, answer 'YES'. If you received a clemency discharge, answer 'NO'.)

This does *not* say "Do you have an honorable discharge?" If you were booted out of the service with a General Discharge, it was under honorable conditions unless it *specifically* stipulates "other than honorable conditions." If you have a "Dishonorable Discharge" or a clemency discharge, you should, of course, investigate getting this changed. Check with the VA or a Veterans' advocacy group.

Item 26: Health Status. "To insure that you are not placed in a position which might impair your health, or which might be a hazard to you or others, we need information about the following:

Do you have, or have you had, heart disease, a nervous break-down, epilepsy, tuberculosis, or diabetes?"

If the above question appears on the SF 171 you are using, get an updated form. This discriminatory question formerly trapped recovered alcoholics who were bent on a confessional. It has been eliminated.

Items 38 through 45: Fines and Terminations. Again it is important to have an updated form. The older forms demand reporting of any traffic fine of $30; now the figure is $100, and subsequent forms may put it higher.

Item 38 states, "During the past ten years, were you fired from any job for any reason, did you quit after being told that you would be fired, or did you leave by mutual consent because of specific problems?" This is an obtuse and very unfair question that I expect will be modified in the future. Nevertheless, there it is.

The person who composed this question obviously regarded the term "fired" to be synonymous with "discharged with extreme prejudice." This is not necessarily the case. The American word "fired" comes from a play on words, in that to discharge a gun and to fire a gun mean the same thing. All employment terminations that are initiated by the employer constitute firing or discharging, even if on the most amicable conditions. Furthermore, everyone actually leaves employment by mutual consent. They stop paying you, so you stop coming to work, or *vice versa*. Review chapter 4 to help with this question.

Item 42: Convictions and Imprisonment. You are reminded that convictions means convictions, not arrests. Item 42 is an attempt to get around this distinction by asking for all forfeiture of collateral, imprisonment, probation, or parole. While the probation or parole inclusions may seem redundant in view of the previous questions on convictions, these are couched to include applicants who have been given a "pretrial diversion" in lieu of indictment. This is an option available to a prosecutor that permits him to offer a defendant a year of probation without trial, after which he will have a clean slate.

Regarding the question on imprisonment, law enforcement officers and prison officials differentiate between jails and prisons, so if you spent a night as a guest of the county, you may decide not to call that "imprisonment."

You are cautioned against outright lying on the SF 171, as it is technically a felony, although no busy U.S. Attorney's office would bother with prosecution unless such a falsification were in support of other more serious crimes. However, if you are hired without being caught in a falsified answer, the application form will be sitting there in your personnel file ready to pounce the moment a superior gets mad enough at you to plot your departure. Discovery of a deliberate falsification in an initial application is a much used gimmick to bypass the protections against arbitrary firing that civil service employees enjoy.

State civil service has many advantages not shared by its federal counterpart. Although the entry level pay is usually much lower, there are many more openings and the possibility of obtaining a job nearby in a reasonable time is good. Promotion to a higher position is usually by competitive examination on general information—an area of knowledge which is usually a piece of cake for recovering alcoholics.

The reason for so many entry level openings in state civil service is that people constantly leave for better jobs if advancement does not present itself quickly. You needn't decide whether to try federal civil service or opt for the state application, as you will file for as many openings as you can possibly qualify for in *both* services.

Wrapping up: You must treat all civil service applications exactly as you would a lottery ticket. You will do your best in filing the forms, then forget them and go about your job search. If you put all your eggs in the civil service basket, the years will surely slip-slide away.

THE MILITARY SERVICE OPTION

The military service should always be considered for younger job seekers. "Joining up" in the military is not as easy as many detractors would have us believe. But if you are so inclined, and can qualify, you will come out in a few short years with salable job skills and experience that will knock your socks off. Low level enlisted men and women learn and work at state-of-the-art computer equipment and programs that a civilian graduate engineer couldn't match in ten years. Spend an hour with the local recruiter. It may be an eye opener, and it doesn't cost a nickel.

WHAT ABOUT SUBSTANCE ABUSE COUNSELING?

Beware the "Johnny Cash" syndrome. Years ago, the warden at Folsom Prison told an interviewer that after an in-prison concert by Johnny Cash and June Carter, counselors couldn't get short-timers to concentrate on any postincarceration vocational plan other than touring prisons with a guitar and entertaining the inmates.

The first vocational idea that comes to many recovered alcoholics and drug addicts is substance abuse-related social service. *I've been down the road. I speak their language. They'll listen to me. I've got a mission to help them.*

"Them," of course, refers to alcoholics or addicts still struggling with their problem. We are reminded of a colleague who was looking for his niche in life after World War II. He had been an intelligence officer, spoke Japanese fluently, and had visions of a lucrative postwar career in the Orient. What he learned, to his dismay, was that there were millions of *native* Japanese ex-servicemen in Japan who had spoken Japanese perfectly from the age of two. Now, if he were an electronics engineer or an industrial chemist, *and* spoke Japanese, he would have been welcome in the Far East.

So it is with "professional alcoholics." There may be some readers of this text who are well-paid, full-time substance abuse counselors, whose only qualification for a counseling position was past addiction. If so, you are either a rare exception or you grandfathered your position early in the game before substance abuse rehabilitation became a major industry.

If you are a doctor or a nurse and a recovered alcoholic, you have much to offer. If you have a graduate degree or extensive training and experience in vocational counseling *and* are a recovered alcoholic, you also may have much to offer. If you have the aptitude, drive, stamina, and resources to pursue further education to get an Associate Degree or Alcoholism Counselor Certification, you have our blessing and encouragement.

But if your sole credentials consist of having been a drunk, you'd best confine your activity in this field to volunteer work within AA or whatever other continuing therapy you have chosen.

There is an old employment service joke about an interviewer who asked an applicant if he knew anything about medicine. "Well, I've been sick a lot." The interviewer then said, "Okay, that ought to supply you with a strong background for this opening in brain surgery."

For those of you determined to enter the field, remember that legitimate rehabilitation institutions will always require evidence of two to five years of continuous sobriety as a firm prerequisite. Success stories are few. Pay is low. Job security is chancy as programs usually depend on year to year grants. For these and other mysterious reasons, the turnover rate in alcoholism counseling is high. (Just ask anyone who has tried to maintain an accurate mailing list of active alcoholism and substance abuse counselors!)

On the other hand, for some illogical reason, some counselors hang in there, year after year, heartbreak after heartbreak. For them, a few outstanding success stories more than make up for miles of gloomy statistics. God Bless them!

7

MAKING THE MOST OF THE INTERVIEW

The job interview is your primary goal. By this time, you should have learned that eternal abstinence is too great a burden for the recovering alcoholic to bear, and so sobriety is achieved one day at a time. Similarly, if your mind is fixed on getting hired, each rejection is seen as a failure and the task becomes overwhelming. Getting an interview, not getting a job, must be your daily goal and the purpose of everything that has gone before. You shoot for an average of two interviews a day, with any abbreviated interviews or cancellations supplanted with alternate "walk-in" cold approaches you have held in reserve.

The first sober interview is always associated with sweaty palms, much pacing back and forth in front of the office, fleeting notions of scrubbing the mission because of a cowlick, or a broken nail, or a moment's difficulty locating the building, or whatever. But then you recall that you have a pocketful of alternate interview targets; targets that you've committed yourself to "cold approach" if this one aborts for any reason. So, what the hell—here goes!

Just before your name is called by the receptionist, a warm feeling of confidence comes over you. You realize that you are probably in better shape than any candidate in the room—maybe in town! Measure these assets against your competition, and *believe* them:

- You're sober, and you don't have a hangover. This might put you one up on most people in the room——including the interviewer.
- You know an interviewer can't hurt you. What can they possibly do to you that you haven't already been through?
- You know something about the company and the job. You aren't worried about how much it pays, because you've already made your minimum salary cut-off decision.
- While it would be great to score the first time out, you're sober enough to know the odds are against this, and what's more, your life doesn't depend on *this* job. You have a hundred other targets in your job search folder, and the prospect list is growing.
- You got an interview! This is what all your preparation has been pointed toward. You're going to find it exciting. You're going to learn from it. You're going to get so damn good at it you'll soon be enjoying every moment you spend in this situation.

So you see, you have an almost unfair advantage over the other candidates in the waiting room. But once your name is called, there are several other tricks you will use to change the odds in your favor. You have from ten to thirty minutes to sell yourself to the employer and find out if you want to work there if the job is offered. Never forget that an interview is a two-way street. It is not a begging exercise, but a negotiation between two parties, *both* of whom are looking for a profitable exchange of talent, skill, time, and money.

ELIMINATE DISTRACTIONS

Considering the amount that has to be accomplished in such a short period, there are a few necessary adjustments in the job seeker's habits. You must eliminate——at least for the brief period of the interview——nervous and distracting practices.

Jewelry

Leave at home, or in your pocket or briefcase, all rings (except wedding), flashy tie pins or other jewelry, novelty or space-age watches, and lodge lapel insignias. The latter item, if quite small and discreet, may be excused if research has shown that the person to whom you will be speaking is an active member of that lodge or fraternity. However, if the interviewer shows you a paid-up lodge card, he is tacitly requesting that the interviewee pull out one too; and there had better be one!

The reasoning behind the elimination of class rings and scuba diving watches is the necessity of jealously concentrating the interviewer's attention on you for every second of the interview. We don't want the interviewer's memory cluttered with visions of gaudy and sparkling things, no matter how much they mean to you or how useful they are to you.

Smoking

DO NOT SMOKE! This admonition has nothing to do with health or morality. For the short period of the interview you can do without. In the first place, more and more people are finding it offensive. Even if the interviewer is smoking, do not smoke. The primary reason for refraining is that a flaming lighter, a burning cigarette, smoke pouring forth from mouth and nostrils and butts grinding into ash trays are spectacularly distracting events when viewed from across the desk. You don't have time for this, so pound this into your head: *in any interview situation, do not smoke!*

Body Distractions

Most people walk into an interview situation dragging seven pesky and unmanageable kids——one body, two legs, two hands, and two eyes. Try this little exercise tonight while you're watching the evening news on TV:

Place a kitchen chair at a comfortable distance from the television. Sit with the lower part of your back flush against the chair back, but not ramrod straight. Both feet are flat on the floor, about sixteen inches apart, with one foot extended a bit ahead of the other. Your hands rest on your legs, cupped in a natural position, with only the side opposite your thumb touching. Adjust the legs and arms to a comfortable position.

This is your "home" position. If you are a typist, you know that no matter what keys you strike, your fingers return to your home position. The same is true with a tennis player, who returns to the same key spot on the court after each return.

You may use your hands when making a point, but when you are through, they will return to their home position. You may lean your body forward to show attentiveness, or back to show reflection, but your butt will remain solid against the chair back. You will not cross and uncross your legs, or engage in the common nervous knee jiggle, because your feet remain flat on the floor.

Now we're ready for the evening news. Peter Jennings, Tom Brokaw, or Dan Rather are the interviewers. The time devoted to these programs is a good practice length for an average interview, with time out for commercials. So, for the time that they or their coanchor people are looking at you, you look at them—straight in the eye. Your hands will not clasp and unclasp or move to the mouth, nose, ears, hair, tie, or glasses.

You may pretend you are handing them a résumé, or emphasizing a reply with a hand gesture, but then your hand will automatically bounce back to its home position. After working at this exercise for a few evenings, you will find that knowing in advance what you are going to do with your legs, hands, body, and eyes leaves much more time to devote to the business at hand. The air of confidence this telegraphs will impress the interviewer, although he or she may not consciously realize this is happening.

SIZE UP YOUR INTERVIEWER

You will soon learn to classify the interviewer as one of four types: talker, listener, troublemaker, or interview machine.

Talkers

You will listen to the talkers, but keep them on the subject. They mustn't be allowed to stray to irrelevant topics. This is *your* time they're burning up. They are getting *paid* to sit there and talk, you're not. Soak up all the information you can about the company as they lay it on, then bring the subject back to *you*, and how *you* fit into the picture.

Listeners

You will talk to the listeners, telling them enough about yourself to show you can handle the job—then stop. You should then start asking pertinent questions about the company and specifics about the position. You shouldn't be afraid to ask questions about pay and benefits, but those questions should be postponed until after intelligent and knowledgeable questions about the operation of the company have been asked. Don't get spooked by "dead air." Many job seekers have talked themselves into a good job and then talked themselves back out of consideration while the interviewer was quietly trying to figure a way to work them into the operation.

Troublemakers

These are usually nonprofessional personnel people who have seen a training film on interview techniques. The only technique they can remember is the stress interview, and they try to use it in every situation. They may throw out a "What would you do if . . . ?" question and wait to see if the applicant squirms, like the subject did in the film. Stress interviews weren't designed for use with recovering alcoholics. You've been under stress interrogations that this guy would think came out of Dante's *Inferno*, and somehow you've always managed to skate through. The textbook answer to most "what if" questions would go like this: "Well, first I'd take immediate action to ensure the safety of the personnel and protection of the equipment, then I'd contact a superior for explicit instructions."

Nonprofessional personnel people—usually job bosses or supervisors pressed into the selection process—are frequently embarrassed by the selection interview and need help. Be ready to give it, without letting them know you are taking charge of the interview. These people will respond to only one kind of flattery: recognition of their knowledge of the job.

Under the influence of increased governmental pressure against job discrimination, many interviewers have come to fear asking any specific questions. "Tell me about yourself." This should be an anticipated and welcome opening to do just that; to give your brief sales pitch about how much you know about the company's operation and how well you would fit into it.

"Where do you see yourself in five years?" Another old standard from a training film on "How to Interview." The interviewer really isn't looking for an informative answer here, so don't shock him or her with something memorable. Interviewers *will* remember replies suggesting a desire to return to school, any threatening ambition, or hints that this job would be only a way-station on the road to greater things. Neither is this a place to announce in righteous feminism that having babies is part of the five-year plan. A simple rhetorical response that will satisfy the simplistic rhetorical question is, "I've learned to take things one day at a time, and absolutely, my only concern for the foreseeable future will be to give this job my very best shot."

A folksy approach by the interviewer should not be taken as a sign that points are being scored. Nonprofessional interviewers will frequently soak up valuable time rambling about the weather or last night's ball game. They must be gently steered back to the subject.

Interview Machines

The Interview Machine is usually a functionary in the employment office of a medium to large operation. When we think of this category we are always reminded of a skit once performed by the comedy team Bob and Ray. Bob Elliott played a State Department official returning from an important mission and the late Ray Goulding was the TV news interviewer who paid absolutely no attention to the answers he was getting, frequently asking a prepared question that had just been answered by Bob in detail.

It is important to ask Interview Machines to include certain important information in the comments section of their form (they will always have a form). Your research and preparation has been designed to get you a little better attention. Therefore, you should never run into an Interview Machine except during a cold approach used as an alternate. Anyhow, the names of the individuals with the authority to make the hiring decision must be pulled out of the interviewer. Then, the Ignition Letter and end-run operation can be put into action.

DEMONSTRATE KNOWLEDGE OF THE COMPANY

As you are now aware, the nonalcoholic competition is numerous and fairly competent, and your job is to change the odds in your favor. One way this is done is through the demonstration of corporate and job knowledge. Few of the other applicants will have researched the company and the specific job with your thoroughness, and the interviewer will feel more comfortable speaking with you because of this.

Always prepare at least two questions showing your knowledge of the industry, that particular company, and that particular job. This little exercise will automatically move you ahead of most of the people in the waiting room.

REMEMBER THEIR NAMES; MAKE THEM REMEMBER YOURS

Another odds-changer is the use of the most intimate knowledge about interviewers available on short notice——their name. Their name *must* be gotten right. If it is an unfamiliar or foreign name, they must be asked to repeat it until the pronunciation is nailed down. Then it must be *used*. It must be salted into the interview at regular and natural intervals, without overdoing it.

A radio sportscaster who covered play-by-play for a major league team used to keep a three-minute sandglass egg timer running beside his mike to remind him to give the score at regular intervals. As interview skills develop, a mental sandglass also will develop to help salt the interviewer's name into the exchange at appropriate points.

The other odds changer that follows naturally is to make the interviewer remember you and *your* name. It is usually considered "uncool" to use old business cards with the former company and phone number blacked out. You may be surprised, however, that by a bit of shopping you can find a very inexpensive source of cards printed with name, address, and phone number. Mail order houses that advertise in family magazines frequently use address labels, business cards, and printed stationery as loss leaders to develop mailing lists.

We have had clients print their names in large, neat, block letters on their résumé folder, casually placing it on the desk so it is facing the interviewer throughout the session. One of our female clients with a distinctive and usually-forgotten name wore a neat and conservative name tag to interviews, pointing to it with a smile as she introduced herself. Of course, interviewers will have the applicant's name in their records as it appears on the form in front of them, but the problem is to make a permanent mental association between the name and the person.

Working a name into an interview without gimmicks and without cluttering the pitch requires skill and planning, but is worthwhile in changing the odds.

E. Z. Duzzit, that's exactly right, Mr. Fister. It's frequently mispronounced, but you said it properly . . . E. Z. Duzzit.

I'm proud to predict that when you check my references they'll say that E. Z. Duzzit was one of the best drafters they had.

I know you have my number, but if you want me in a hurry, E. Z. Duzzit is in the book."

COVER STORIES

As you are well aware by now, my rule of thumb when dealing
with the question of confessionals on applications and résumés is
"When in doubt, don't." This is especially true during interviews.
Sometimes, the questioning may start zeroing in on your past
problems, and you may be tempted to blurt out a disclosure that
is unwarranted, unnecessary, and terminal.

Even if you are determined to use a cover story to patch over
a particular bad period of your life, you must avoid fabrication if
possible, avoid instant fabrication absolutely, and never, never,
volunteer a cover story! *Very few qualified people have blown an
interview by what they didn't say.*

This matter was covered earlier in the book, but while we're
on the subject of interviews, it bears repeating. Although the
decision to consider or reject a cover story is a very personal
matter, it is a decision you will make eventually. Please factor
these items into your equation:

Cover stories are carefully planned alternate histories that are
well-researched, backstopped, used only in extreme emergency,
and *never volunteered*. If the interviewer wants to know exactly
what you did between 1980 and 1982 when you were serving time,
on the bum, or in the Home for Bewildered Veterans, you should
make him ask just that question. "Precisely where were you and
exactly what did you do during the entire period between January
1, 1980 and December 31, 1982." Only then might the invocation
of a carefully prepared cover story be considered, and then only
within the strict confines discussed in the earlier chapters.

AFTER THE INTERVIEW

When you've given your best shot, and sense that the interview is
over, assist the interviewer in ending it. Recap your qualifications,
reiterate your conviction that you'll be able to contribute to the
organization, ask when a decision will be made, repeat the
interviewer's name, repeat your own name, thank the interviewer,
and depart.

After leaving the interview room, possibly in the reception area, some quick-written notes should be made on that company's target sheet. That's what the interviewer is doing——jotting down impressions of you, so when they call you back for a second look the interviewer or his or her partner can pick up where they left off. You must have the same advantage, so write it down.

> *3/15/92: Interviewed by Personnel Director Feeney P. Fister (short, balding, rimless specs, Southern accent); seemed interested in my schematic drawings of kibblers. Said Plant Manager T. T. Topdog would make decision by the end of month.*

A follow-up "Thank You" note should be sent within a few days of the interview. This reinforces your name and face in the interviewer's memory, and is another apparently corny device with a track record of working.

Mark your calendar for a follow-up call and letter on the decision date that was extracted from the interviewer. If the follow-up suggests that they have not yet made up their minds, you should ask if you can help the process along by adding additional information, or coming in for a supplemental interview. You will try again for a decision date, and mark that on your calendar for a follow-up.

Finally, if you are told by phone or letter that the company decided to select someone else, you'll write them another thank you note for the courtesies extended during their consideration. There will be other job openings at that company, personnel people exchange information, and personnel people change companies. *Always leave them loving you.*

8

WORK AN EIGHT-HOUR DAY

Working *an eight-hour day also applies to job search.*

The term "Work Ethic" has been defiled and reduced to a pejorative joke by recent generations of intellectual failures. Our parents spoke with pride of "giving an honest day's work for an honest day's pay." Much of the guilt and fear associated with a recovered alcoholic's job search can be traced to recognition of years of constantly violating that code.

As you have undoubtedly observed, most alcoholics have always subscribed to the standard of putting forth their best effort —of an honest day's work, in other words. While the active phase of the disease suppresses this tenet, those of you who have suffered through it will remember residual indications. When you watched a football or baseball game, you soon identified and zeroed in on any player you deemed not giving his best and pulling his weight. If you were in a hospital or rehab, this extended to your observations of employees of that institution——including counselors!

If your therapy included chores such as cleaning up the day room, you will recall that your strongest derogatories were reserved for the fellow inmate who was goofing off. Recovering alcoholics always fall short of their own high standards of performance. The remorse that follows the realization of not doing a good job is part of the misery cycle of active alcoholism. Let's discuss, for a moment, the necessity of an honest day's work in your job search efforts.

While working with unemployed veterans returning to an impoverished inner city that resembled some bombed-out villages overseas, I made a chilling observation. Through analysis of literally thousands of case histories it became apparent that we had a window of about six weeks to be effective. During that short period after discharge, we had to convince the veteran to make an educational or vocational decision and move on it, or he probably would be trapped in the slum of his childhood for the rest of his life.

The attitude we had to break down resembled alcoholism, in that it fed upon itself and received the protection and encouragement of well-meaning but ignorant family and friends. *Get a job? Later man. Right now I need some time to 'get it all together'.* If it took longer than six weeks to "get it all together," he had bought a 1980 "deuce-and-a-quarter" Buick, was paying the finance company twenty-five dollars a week forever, his girlfriend was pregnant, he had a court appearance coming up, he had spent his mustering-out pay, he had made a drug contact and was starting to slither into a habit he had only experimented with in the service, and the party was over.

Then, he comes into the employment office——still wearing parts of his uniform——and says, "Man, I need a job right now, and I'll take anything." And that's just what he gets. Anything. So long, job counselor. Hello, social worker and probation officer.

You must be prepared to work harder getting a job than you expect to work after you are hired. This is important for the success of your quest. It is imperative for your own mental health and that of your family. The recovered alcoholic who sends out five hundred résumé s, then sits at home reading the want ads, soon becoming engrossed in the tortured tribulations of *All My Children* and *Days of Our Lives*, is playing to lose. Waiting for the phone to ring with a job offer or the mail to deliver a report-for-work notice is stupid and dishonest.

Every man and woman who reads this book is subject to this charge. Repeat it loud and long, until you get the message:

Set your alarm each morning and be showered, dressed, and at the breakfast table by seven-thirty.

If you take a morning paper, it should be scanned for new job openings. After the first week of familiarization, that scanning should take no longer than ten minutes.

By eight-thirty you go to work. No browsing through the sports section or fashion ads over a third cup of coffee. If you want to do that, be at the breakfast table by seven o'clock.

No watching the second half of the *Today* show. No excuses about waiting for the mail. You must get to work! You have the toughest boss in the world——You!

If you are in the target selection or scanning major papers stage, you should be at the library the moment they open the doors.

If you have an interview in the afternoon, either spend the morning boning up on the company and product in the library and collecting data for additional Ignition Letters, or making a "cold approach" request for an interview from your list of alternate targets.

When the working day is over, you rest——not before. You collect your thoughts about the day that was given to you and what you did with it.

If you had an interview or got a promise of two interviews or more, it was a very good day. If you had two interviews and got three lined up, it was a terrific day.

Now, rest. Play with the kids. Have some sober fun. Enjoy being available to help someone. Go to an AA or NA meeting. Let your batteries recharge. Sleep. Because tomorrow you're going to be given another day.

And you're going to be working eight hours of that day. You've got a damn tough boss.

DOWN TIME, DISAPPOINTMENTS, AND ELATION

You and those around you know or are beginning to suspect that the recovered alcoholic is a package of riddles. Time is both your friend and your enemy. You've learned what time and perseverance can do in changing you from an impossible job candidate into a viable applicant. John Milton's sonnet on his blindness ends, "They also serve who only stand and wait," but in an alcoholic's eyes, they who stand and wait are also served.

The Waiting Game

Alcoholics cannot just stand or sit and wait. This is a difficult occupation for "normal" people. It is an absurd assignment for a newly recovered alcoholic. Bars and cocktail lounges are strategically located to preclude the terrible contingency of having to just stand and wait. There is a bar everywhere a gap in planned activities occurs. That's why they are at airports, train stations, bus terminals, hotel lobbies, restaurant waiting areas, theater lounges, and across the street from personnel offices. "I'll wait for you at the bar." "Is that today's paper, bartender? I have a little time to kill."

So many recovering alcoholics start their job search in the morning bright and early with smiles on their faces, interview appointments lined up and fresh impressive résumé tucked in their briefcases, only to come home drunk. Alcoholics have a bomb ticking away inside that must be periodically reset or it will go off. That is why you are taught in rehab and self-help programs to stay away from people, places and things that might cause you to pick up a drink.

The following scenario is unfortunately repeated often, every day of the week, around the country. The alcoholic arrives downtown for a job interview an hour early. He has two cups of coffee, and the table server has picked up his cup, wiped off his table, and given him his check. If he stalls twenty seconds, she is back with a sarcastic, "Will there be anything else, SIR?" He pays up and leaves, possibly stopping at another coffee shop to soak up some time and sharpen his nerves.

Finally the appointment time is approaching. The employer had told him to telephone a half hour before coming in, to make sure he hadn't been called away to a meeting. Now, our alcoholic has a bladder full of breakfast coffee, plus the three cups he's had downtown. Who has a restroom that is in plain view and can be used without asking permission? Why, only the "friendly tavern," of course. After he's relieved himself, he walks back into the familiar surroundings. Taverns were made for waiting.

There is the telephone. He has to get some change, so he buys a Coke. The call to the employer brings an apology from the receptionist. The employer will be in a meeting all morning, but he may be able to spare a few minutes at two o'clock. Now our alcoholic sits down with his Coke and feels a little silly.

Alcoholics Anonymous has a "Murphy's Law" saying that bears repeating here: "If you're an alcoholic with a Coke and sit next to a beer drinker at a bar, he'll have you drinking beer before you have him drinking Coke." Five, four, three, two, one——lift off.

All of this was predictable and could have been avoided with intelligent planning. Strategic loafing spots must be located around town as carefully as a spy would check out a clandestine meeting place. Libraries are recommended for all the reasons stated earlier, including their telephones and clean toilets. Almost every medium-sized city has at least one Alcoholics Anonymous-oriented club room that is ideal for loafing.

Start every day with an ample supply of telephone and subway change. There may be plenty of reasons for going into a bar, but for alcoholics, never an excuse. As soon as you find yourself in a waiting situation, you must spot the public toilets. You used to think the only restrooms available to the public in the world were in taverns and cocktail lounges, and it is embarrassing to go into a business establishment and use their "facility" without buying something. Your new headquarters, the library, will have a restroom, of course. But there are also accommodations in all large department stores, although the use of the latter is discouraged by placing them in a back corner of the fifth or sixth floor. For early use, you will check out the bus station, a hotel lobby, the court house or municipal building basements, and you'll learn which filling stations in the area leave the side restrooms unlocked.

Alternate Planning

You will never leave home for an interview unless you have at least four "cold-approach" targets set up as alternates. If you walk in for your morning appointment, only to have the secretary say it's been cancelled, you immediately schedule another appointment, and depart for your first alternate target.

Last-minute cancellations are extremely dangerous for the alcoholic job seeker. A half-dozen "slip" catalysts are simultaneously triggered into action. You have your adrenalin up for the interview, but in the back of your mind you fear the impending confrontation and the possibility of an embarrassing rejection. When, at the last moment, you learn of the postponement or cancellation, you receive it with a mixture of disappointment, self-pity, mock anger, and guilty relief. You fantasize about how the interview might have gone. Add to these emotions a sudden, unexpected few hours of time on your hands. *Crisis!*

A recovered alcoholic or addict must never leave these secondary targets to chance. Never say to yourself, "I'll pick one out of the paper or Yellow Pages if the occasion arises." These alternates must be in your armory along with crib sheets and résumés when you leave home every morning.

Expect the unexpected. Little disturbances in daily routines are dangerous. A flat tire, a missed bus, a cancelled appointment, coffee spilled on the one-and-only interview suit, the frustration of being summarily rejected for a job you thought you had wrapped up—these are frightening occurrences for substance abusers, whether they are actively into their addictions or recovering. They can trigger tragedy, and they will happen, in some form or other, during a job search.

So will pleasant surprises, which can be equally dangerous. People with addictive personalities are particularly vulnerable during periods of elation. It is tempting, after a terrific interview, to call it a day. You must remind yourself early and often that you are working an eight-hour day. The best way to make productive use of that "high" is to carry it right into your next planned or alternate interview.

Robert Frost wrote of reluctantly leaving a woods filling up with snow on a dark evening because he had "promises to keep." One blessed fringe benefit of sobriety is being able, at long last, to make and keep promises. Promises can be an added insurance policy during this critical stage of your life: a promise to meet someone at an AA or NA meeting; a promise to take the kids to a dairy bar for a milk shake; a promise to be home early for supper with a sober smile. A promise that the day will be judged by having done your best, by having gotten some interviews, by having learned something, and by staying straight and sober— nothing else.

9

LABOR LAWS:
WHAT YOU MUST KNOW

Recovered alcoholics should be aware of a few matters of labor law.

In an earlier chapter we discussed a few legal protections recovered alcoholics have against unfair employment practices by certain employers. I also mentioned that it might not be a bed of roses working for a small company that was forced to hire you.

Laws against discrimination in employment based on a worker's history of alcoholism or drug abuse are extremely controversial. They are considered by many detractors to be the ultimately ridiculous "affirmative action" in a long list of regulated hiring practices imposed on American business.

I am only discussing federal laws concerning employment of alcoholics. Many states have similar laws that would offer broader coverage, and for this information you will want to check with your state alcoholism information office. The acts of primary interest are:

- Comprehensive Alcohol Abuse and Alcoholism Prevention, Treatment, and Rehabilitation Act of 1970.
- Vocational Rehabilitation Act of 1973.

The Comprehensive Alcoholism Act covers discrimination in federal civil service and licensing: "TITLE II, Section 201 — Alcohol Abuse and Alcoholism Among Federal Civilian Employees. (c)(1) No person may be denied or deprived of Federal civilian employment or a Federal professional or other license or right solely on the ground of prior alcohol abuse or prior alcoholism. (2) This subsection shall not apply to employment (A) in the Central Intelligence, the Federal Bureau of Investigation, the National Security Agency, or any other department or agency of the Federal Government designated for purposes of national security by the President, or (B) in any position in any department or agency of the Federal Government, not referred to in clause (A), which position is determined pursuant to regulations prescribed by the head of such agency or department to be a sensitive position . . .. This title shall not be construed to prohibit the dismissal from employment of a Federal civilian employee who cannot properly function in the employment."

The wise, sober alcoholic will discuss these protections carefully with a trusted counselor before charging forward, righteous sword of retribution in hand. The screwed-up thinking process of the active or temporarily-dry alcoholic will be magnetically attracted to the imagined clout he or she perceives in section (c) (1) above. In actual practice, this would only be beneficial if the alcoholic could prove that he was being denied a civil service appointment solely on a history of alcoholism.

The civil service selection mechanism is so competitive that the hiring agency rarely must give a reason for nonselection other than that of choosing a more desirable candidate. Furthermore, you will note in (2) above that all agencies that actually would run intensive background investigations are exempt from the provisions of the law.

Assuming you are not applying for one of those exempt positions, any information regarding your past alcohol abuse probably came directly or indirectly from leads you yourself provided on the application form. If you are bidding on a civil service job at a reasonable level, and are well-qualified, and are convinced that you are being denied consideration because of a *history* of alcoholism, this information may well have come to their attention through one of your references.

History was italicized, to emphasize that it is presumed you are now sober. You will have checked your own references, so you should not be surprised that one of your former employers has been reporting on past drinking problems.

About a month after the closing date of the announcement for the position, you should query the office mentioned in the announcement regarding the status of your application. As soon as you are informed that another candidate was selected, you may begin the complaint process.

HOW TO FILE A COMPLAINT

Under the Office of Personnel Management (OPM), which now has the responsibility for civil service in the federal system, there is a branch known as the Office of Special Counsel. It is separate and autonomous from the other divisions involved in selection and operations. Any complaint regarding improper selection practices would be filed with this office. Address your letter to:

Office of Special Counsel (OPM)
1717 H Street NW
Washington, DC 20419

You will inform them of your complaint by certified mail. The letter should be short and succinct, such as:

The purpose of this letter is to file a formal complaint. I believe that I have been denied federal employment because of a prior and no longer extant condition of alcoholism in violation of title II, Section 201, of the Comprehensive Alcohol Abuse and Alcoholism Prevention, Treatment, and Rehabilitation Act of 1970, and the Vocational Rehabilitation Act of 1973 as amended.

You will follow this with basic identifying data on the position applied for, ask for an immediate and thorough investigation, and STOP. You will be given an opportunity to supply relevant evidence in the course of the investigation, but this is not the time to lay out all the cards. You also will want to send a copy of your complaint to the National Institute on Alcohol Abuse and Alcoholism, Rockville, MD 20850.

A long delay or an apparently perfunctory investigation should be prodded through a polite letter to your Senator or U.S. Representative. Bureaucrats will swear that these "congressional inquiries" make no impression and delay the investigative process; however, in truth, this is just wishful thinking.

All congressional mail must be answered and answered immediately. These answers must include reasons for delay, some sort of timetable, or an acceptable explanation for unfavorable findings. But please, give them a fair chance to conduct the investigation on their own before shaking them up with a congressional inquiry, as these external proddings generate loads of paperwork and tend to irritate the investigator.

Within the *Vocational Rehabilitation Act of 1973*, you are concerned with two sections—503 and 504. Section 503, in very simplified terms, declares that every employer doing business with the federal government under a contract for more than $2500 must take "affirmative action" to hire handicapped people. Contracts may be for the procurement of supplies, or for the use of real or personal property.

"Affirmative action" covers more than hiring. It also provides protection in the fields of job assignments, promotions, training, transfers, working conditions, terminations, and so on.

Since coverage under this section extends to subcontractors and subsidiaries of contractors, nearly half the businesses in America—some four million—are covered.

Section 504 covers institutions that are getting federal financial assistance and states that they must take steps to assure that handicapped people are not discriminated against in employment. Included are schools, colleges, hospitals, nursing homes, social service agencies, and many more kinds of institutions and establishments—including nearly all state and local agencies.

We also should mention the *Vietnam Era Veterans Readjustment Assistance Act of 1974*, which includes similar provisions to protect disabled veterans receiving compensation from the Veterans Administration at a rate of thirty percent or more; however, since the regulations covering this Act are nearly identical to those of Section 503 and are enforced by the same agency, separate treatment would be redundant.

A well-publicized Supreme Court decision in 1988 that discussed "willful misconduct" and "the disease of alcoholism" addressed a special situation and did not affect these laws.

The matter of affirmative action for recovered alcoholics was addressed publicly by the government through a Department of Labor news release on July 6, 1977. It created a flurry of press reaction——almost all negative. Major columnists wrote on the subject, editorials blasted away, and editorial cartoonists had a field day depicting employers being forced to hire drunks ahead of qualified applicants. Here is the item that sparked the controversy:

FEDERAL CONTRACTORS REMINDED THAT EEO LAW COVERS ALCOHOLICS, DRUG ABUSERS

Alcoholics and drug abusers are covered by the Labor Department's equal employment opportunity (EEO) program for handicapped workers . . . federal government contractors and subcontractors were reminded today.

Under the law . . . employers with a contract or subcontract of $2,500 or more are prohibited from employment discrimination against qualified handicapped persons. These employers must also take affirmative action, or positive steps, to hire and promote qualified handicapped workers.

The law is enforced by the department's Employment Standards Administration, Office of Federal Contract Compliance Programs. Specifically, (the pertinent Section) covers persons who (1) have a physical or mental impairment which substantially limits one or more life activities, (2) have a record of such impairment, or (3) are regarded as having such an impairment.

Although some employers have been uncertain about whether alcoholics and drug abusers are considered handicapped, it is clear . . . that Congress, in enacting the 1973 Rehabilitation Act, fully intended to cover these two groups.

Employers who fail to consider qualified alcoholics and drug abusers for employment because of their handicap (according to the Department spokesperson) are clearly violating the spirit of that law.

Federal contractors and subcontractors found in violation of the law and its implementing regulations may be debarred from government contract work, have their contracts terminated, or the government may take them to court.

Our government spends a considerable amount of money each year to rehabilitate alcoholics and drug abusers, to help them again become employable, productive citizens, (the Department of Labor spokesperson added), and it would be incongruous to turn around and deny them protection under the antidiscrimination law.

The (Department spokesperson) explained, however, that the enforcement program emphasizes the term 'qualified,' and that contractors are expected to take affirmative action to hire and promote only qualified handicapped workers.

Never ones to let facts get in the way of a headline-grabbing issue, the media loosed a vitriolic barrage that, along with the resultant public outcry, forced the Department of Labor into a defensive position. Letters were sent to all major papers, restating the position in the original news release——that the key word was "qualified," and that no contractor would be asked to hire a worker who was currently incapacitated through drug and alcohol abuse, and therefore unqualified.

I was curious whether the government had maintained that position through the intervening decade, and so posed the question to the Secretary of Labor, generating the following response:

US DEPARTMENT OF LABOR
Employment Standards Administration
Office of Federal Contract Compliance Programs

This is in response to your letter to the Secretary of Labor, Elizabeth Dole, concerning recent experience and current policy regarding implementation and enforcement of Section 503 of the Rehabilitation Act of 1973, as amended.

In reference to your question concerning recovered alcoholics and substance abusers, our policy is that companies doing business with the Federal Government must provide equal employment opportunity for qualified handicapped workers. As you know, affirmative action for alcoholics and drug abusers does not require employment of individuals who are unqualified. However, contractors must provide the opportunity for qualified handicapped individuals to compete for employment if reasonable accommodations to their handicap can be made. Specifically, Congress included coverage of alcoholics and drug abusers in amendments to the Rehabilitation Act of 1973 under Public Law 95-602 dated November 6, 1978. That amendment requires that a person whose dependency on alcohol or drugs interferes with acceptable behavior or ability to meet normal job requirements is not a qualified individual within the meaning of the Act. However, if the use of alcohol or controlled substance does not interfere with the individual's job performance, such person may be protected by Section 503.

We are pleased to provide you with a summary of Section 503 activities for Fiscal Year 1988. Thank you for your interest in OFCCP.

Sincerely,
(signed) Leonard J. Biermann, Acting Director

A review of the 1988 summary mentioned above indicated that the Department of Labor's enforcement emphasis in the entire field of affirmative action for all handicapped workers is down to less than ten percent of the 1978 figure. You can imagine how much of that reduced effort is devoted to complaints of alcoholism discrimination.

For the sober alcoholic, it should be plain that legal remedies are a last resort. These laws prohibit discrimination against job applicants and employees by federal contractors and grant recipients when that discrimination is based *solely* on alcoholism or drug abuse. While the regulations do not specify *past* abuse, nor do they stipulate that the abuser must be totally rehabilitated, the overriding factor remains: *The person must be qualified.*

If abusers' drinking or drug use can cause safety or performance problems, they are not qualified. If their disease-inspired behavior creates problems on the job, they are not qualified. If their dependency on alcohol or drugs interferes with acceptable behavior or disturbs their co-workers, they are not qualified. In other words, if you are still drinking or taking drugs, you are not qualified.

Recovered alcoholics or drug abusers have certain protections in employment, but no privileges. They can't wear their disease like a badge of honor and expect preferential treatment. Also, the Act was amended in 1978 to exclude from protection those job applicants and employees who are shown to be currently and actively involved in alcohol and other drug abuse.

Nevertheless, if you believe that you are well-qualified for a position with an employer doing business with the federal government, and that you have been denied employment solely due to past problems with alcohol or drugs, you may wish to file a complaint.

The authority that enforces Section 503 is the Office of Federal Contract Compliance Programs (OFCCP). They have an office in each of the ten Department of Labor regions, and can be found in the phone book under "U.S. Government" in Boston, New York, Philadelphia, Atlanta, Chicago, Kansas City, Dallas, Denver, San Francisco, and Seattle. A letter addressed to their national office will be forwarded to the proper regional headquarters if you are unsure of the regional borders:

Office of Federal Contract Compliance Programs
Handicapped Workers Programs
Employment Standards Administration
U. S. Department of Labor
200 Constitution Ave.
Washington, DC 20210

While the Section 504 complaints (those covering institutions) are investigated by different agencies depending on the department controlling the grant, the OFCCP will take care of proper forwarding of any complaints.

Always remember that legal recourse is to be used as a hole card, not a club.

Part Two

JOB SEARCH
WHEN POVERTY HAS BEEN
AN UNCONSCIOUS OPTION

10

THE THREE TENTS OF TRIAGE

The popluation of alcoholics and drug addicts being treated by rehabilitation centers and released into the world of work has a different look than it did in our parents' time. Back then, drunks who were veterans went to the VA hospital, rich drunks went to fancy drying-out spas, blue collar drunks were treated by their family doctors, and poor drunks were scraped up off the street and sent to public mental wards or died in jail.

Alcoholics Anonymous was founded by a stock broker and a physician. The personal stories in the early editions of the AA "Big Book" were about people who had fallen from their successful perches because of alcohol abuse, and who recovered through AA.

Now we are beginning to see a much wider range of alcoholics being given the advantage of formal recovery programs and professional addiction counseling. People are appearing in aftercare programs and AA and NA beginners meetings who have never had a job, whose parents never had a job, whose grandparents attained welfare status in midlife, and who don't even know anybody who has legal employment.

Others simply became addicted at or before the age when one is expected to make work or education decisions; going directly from adolescence to vagrant, or depending on a former spouse or family to support them and their disease.

The term "recovery" assumes something has been found which has been lost——that one has returned to a previous happy, joyous, and free life style. The last thing these new additions to the work force want to do is "recover" in that sense. Recover to what? What they are looking for is a rebirth.

This part of the book is directed to you job-seekers who have been slapped with the labels "Chronically Unemployed" and "Discouraged Work Force." Society has apparently given up on you. But, if you have the guts and gumption to read this book, you probably have the capability to get over and get out of the poverty category. And we are not going to talk down to you. If you have problems with some words or concepts, you will have to get used to using a dictionary and asking for help. You won't find this reading any more difficult than the sports page or the *TV Guide*.

Nevertheless, these first two chapters in Part II are primarily for job seekers who are working with counselors. If you are making this trip out of poverty on your own and have a tremendous urgency to get started, you may decide to skim through to chapter 11, although I hope you come back and read these remarks again later.

Billions of dollars have been spent on government programs in the past fifty years to place the chronically unemployed in permanent jobs. This money was funnelled down through generations of alphabet-soup agencies to community groups who could convince the government donors that they had the talent and facilities to run a successful job training and placement program.

To ensure the continuous refunding of their programs——and ultimately their own jobs——managers of these placement activities have always been forced to grind out an endless ransom of placement statistics for the sponsoring governmental bureaucracy. At first, these frontline referral agencies usually believed wholeheartedly in the principles they professed in their grant proposals.

But sooner or later, the survival of their project became the name of the game, and many managers of counseling centers developed into extremely adept players. Placements were hungrily recorded on the flimsiest evidence, and credit taken for all jobs gotten by registrants whether the facility had anything to do with getting them the job or not.

Then the inevitable happened. Pressure for success became so oppressive and competition between subcontractors so fierce that more shortcuts were taken, and the line of legality was crossed. Program administrators around the country found themselves subjects of federal prosecution for filing false reports and defrauding the government.

One of many buzz words that developed during the early innocence of these programs was "creaming." In the highly competitive field of job placement and training, "creaming" was a put down term. It referred to the practice of taking credit for easy placements, and ignoring service to the neediest of the needy, the poorest of the poor, and the least likely to succeed.

The "creamers" (those oily rascals!) made a studied effort to recruit into their programs individuals who seemed a little smarter, a bit more educated, already possessing certain job skills or at least with some work experience, who were *already* motivated to move up and out of their present circumstances. What upset the advisory boards at the county and state levels was that job seekers in these categories probably could have obtained employment by simply registering at the Job Service and being referred for an interview.

The real purpose of the programs, the government maintained, was to train, motivate, and place in employment that waxy buildup of souls, sometimes two or three generations deep, who had fallen through the cracks of assistance systems already in place. They asserted that those programs that engaged in "creaming" were achieving their job placement goals by grabbing the easy clients, thus guaranteeing the security of their own jobs.

But what of the managers, administrators, intake interviewers, and counselors who understood and believed in the high purpose of these programs and were determined to play by the stringent spirit of the rules?

Many nights we've driven past their offices. We have seen the lights burning and observed dedicated counselors working late without paid overtime. They were striving to make sense out of a no-win policy. This policy dictated that nearly all of their limited time, effort, talent, physical assets, training facilities and money must be expended on a segment of their clientele that had proved time after time after time that it would *not* respond to this type of attention.

Compassionate zeal combined with unfeeling reality in a cruel dilemma. We watched helplessly as the fire of dedication in one after another fine, young counselor burned low and whimpered out. Don Quixote dreamed impossible dreams, fought unbeatable foes, and died struggling against insurmountable odds. He was an honorable man. He was also crazy as an outhouse mouse.

We have heard substance abuse counselors describe the insanity of addiction in terms of continuously pursuing a plan of action that has a proven record of failure. In the forties, before the concerns of animal lovers had to be considered, researchers in clinical psychology found they could induce psychoses in laboratory animals. The easiest method of causing a healthy animal to develop severe mental illness was through unrelenting frustration.

A male would be placed in a cage with a female in heat, but when he attempted to approach, he would be hit with ice water. Food would be made available, but touching the container would produce a painful shock. Every normal activity would be consciously frustrated until the animal became a quivering wreck.

This week I received an invitation to a weekend seminar for halfway house directors. One workshop was entitled "Counselor Burnout." Counselors, laboratory monkeys, crazy Spanish knights; all continuously pursuing plans of action that have a proven record of failure.

If it appears to you that society has given up on seriously trying to get you up and out of poverty and into productive employment you may be partially right. But it isn't because many people haven't tried. They simply spread themselves too thin, trying to bring every person living below the poverty level up to middle income bracket at the same time; everyone marching along together in a long straight line.

WHAT IS TRIAGE?

The French word "triage" (tree-ahj) developed from the method of sorting battlefield casualties in the Franco-Prussian War. Three tents were set up behind the lines to receive the wounded. A doctor or nurse gave each new arrival a preliminary examination, then directed that they be taken to one of these tents.

In the first tent, the less serious cases were patched up and sent back to the front lines. The second tent was set up to prepare patients for evacuation to field hospitals in the rear where surgery or other procedures could be performed. The third tent contained cots, a nurse to dispense heavy doses of opium and brandy, and a priest to administer last rites.

While the third tent of the triage contained the dreadfully and painfully wounded and naturally would attract the most voluntary attention from compassionate professionals, the practical French realized that concentrating their limited assets on the third tent would neither maximize survivors nor aid the war effort.

God bless the nurses, priests, social workers, and other specialists who dedicate their lives to ministering in the third tent of physical or vocational poverty. Occasionally there are miraculous recoveries in the third tent, but these are unexpected events. Those saints recognize their mission as one of mercy and grace, and their primary goal is comfort, not medical healing or vocational recovery. God bless them.

But that's their job. Some counselors think it's their job, too, and they spend their careers at well-meaning poverty programs tilting at the windmills of terrible odds, until they are eventually consumed.

Unless a job counselor is self-employed, works for a private employment agency, or considers counseling merely a hobby, he or she does not have the luxury of picking and choosing clientele. This is fitting and proper, as I know of no counselors so smart that they can predict success or failure based solely on early encounters with clients. Everyone who comes to their desks must be given the opportunity to take full advantage of their time and skills. They should use every trick in their bags to drag their clients kicking and screaming into the first two tents. When this fails they should ask their colleagues to take a shot, in earnest hope that they have missed an opening.

But somewhere along the line, they surely must recognize when a cultural casualty has settled comfortably and forever into the third tent. Nevertheless, their job descriptions dictate continued routine service to everybody equally. And the lines of new wounded keep coming.

If you find yourself lying on a cot in the third tent of poverty with a priest leaning over you administering Last Rites, it's time to jump out of that death bed and crawl on your hands and knees into a recovery tent. Shout out loud, "I DON'T BELONG HERE. DAMMIT, I'M READING A BOOK! I CARE ABOUT MY-SELF. I'M NOT GOING TO DIE IN THIS TENT. I'M GOING TO BE A SURVIVOR!"

VOCATIONAL VIRGINS

Many of you, even though clean, sober, mentally healthy and physically fit, are extremely improbable candidates for employment. You may be *vocational virgins*. A vocational virgin may be a girl who dropped out of high school to have a baby, or a homemaker forced by circumstance of divorce, widowhood or hard times to enter the employment market for the first time at an older age.

Maybe you are a man who never worked more than a few weeks at any job, and are surrounded by so many kindred souls that you have begun to accept your situation as normal. Or possibly you are stuck in a hopeless rut of waiting. Waiting for the steel mills to start up again. Waiting for the coal mines to start hiring. Waiting for something—anything—good to happen. Your friendly labor statistician has lumped all of you under the umbrella of "disadvantaged."

You don't need any lectures about why poverty happens, or how the system has betrayed you. Politicians and self-proclaimed ethnic or cultural "leaders" have fed you that pap for years in the necessary effort to maintain you as a loyal constituency. You have to deal with the person in the mirror. Today. Now. A real live person with a real live situation.

I don't know why God made poor people. Our height, our skin color, our athletic ability, our musical talent, the city we were born in——that stuff was all just laid on us gratuitously. We all start with what we are, where we are, with what we have. This isn't good, and it isn't bad. It just is. And we can sit on our little pity pots and bitch our lives away if that's our bag.

But it isn't necessary. Though we can't change the cards we've been dealt, the way we play them can make a world of difference. Being poor and having to struggle for a living may be the hand we've been dealt, and that's the hand we'll play. But the game is more akin to draw poker than "showdown." We can trade in some cards and sweeten our hand.

We've all met folks living in unhappy circumstances who wear their poverty like a badge of honor. They use "pride" as a defense mechanism and tell themselves and others that they are proud to be what they are and where they are, whatever the depth of their condition. Pride is conceit, vanity, arrogance, vainglory, self-importance, insolence, haughtiness, snobbishness, superciliousness, hauteur, presumption, and much more; mostly negative.

Yet, all our lives we are taught to be "proud" of things we really had nothing to do with. "Proud" to be an American, a woman, Polish, young, black, Texan, or bald. "Proud" that our ancestors came over on the Mayflower, or as slaves, or as political refugees. We might as well be "proud" that it's raining or that today is Wednesday. Let's face it: ninety-nine percent of us got to America the same way——through our momma's belly. And she may or may not have been "proud" of that.

And we're not going to dwell on the fantasy of getting rich. Great wealth is *always* accidental. I don't mean comfortable living, or even *very* comfortable living, but outrageous, ostentatious opulence. It is ALWAYS accidental. The accident of being born to wealthy parents. The accident of being born with spectacular beauty, amazing physical skills, or an I.Q. that would knock your eyes out. The accident of having show biz talent, and the accident of being in exactly the right place at the right time to be discovered by the right person. Or the blind luck of hitting the lottery.

Of course, most rich and famous people will claim they got there on their own, through courage and hard work. Courage and fortitude help; they help a lot. But real fame and fortune begin with accidents that the rich and famous had nothing to do with.

And while great wealth is accidental, unless you have an incapacitating mental illness or retardation, or suffer from severe total physical disability, poverty is almost always optional. Not just being poor and having to work hard for a living, but *poverty*. Total, miserable, bottomless, hopeless, permanent, wretched *POVERTY*.

A couple of years ago I was sitting in a barber shop in an Appalachian town whose only source of jobs, the coal mine, had been closed for over a year. Besides the barber and a handful of city and state employees, the unemployment rate was one hundred percent. Among the well-thumbed magazines on the bench was a copy of *Newsweek* that featured an article on poverty in America."

On the cover was a ragged little woebegone ragamuffin who looked like she'd been pulled through a chimney. My bench partner studied the picture, spat a stream of Red Man at a coffee can situated there for that purpose, and observed, "Thet ain't no poor little girl; thet's a *dirty* little girl!"

Often, for very good reasons, poor vocational virgins and perpetually unemployed people do not recognize the options available to them. In other cases, for what they earnestly believe are very good reasons, they will not be willing to accept these options. Some sociologists have been trying to work a factor into the government's unemployment figures that they call the "discouraged worker"——one no longer in the labor market because he is tired of looking for just the right job.

A decade or so ago I was working in an area where it was fashionable to listen to Radio Moscow on short wave. One popular late-night program was "Moscow Mailbag." The simple format consisted of a congenial announcer with a comfortable American accent reading letters from listeners in America and answering questions about life in the Soviet Union.

Unemployment in the United States was in the double digits then, and at least one letter an evening asked about the employment situation in Russia. "Unemployment is one of the natural by-products of capitalism," the announcer would piously intone. "In the Soviet Union, as in other 'socialist' countries, there is no unemployment. Everyone who is able to work is assured a job."

That was true, as far as it went. What the Soviet Union and other "socialist" countries did, of course, was to enforce acceptance of the government's choice of: (1) pay level, (2) vocation, (3) working hours and working conditions, (4) job location, (5) family separation, (6) delayed upward mobility (if the possibility existed at all), and (7) total sacrifice of the freedom to say, "Take this job and shove it!" Those of us who have worked many years in the employment field realize that 100 percent employment can occur only when the worker is divested of the liberty to change jobs.

Most employment counselors have occasionally wished they could *force*-feed some of their undermotivated clients with the acceptance of just a few of those Soviet-style conditions. But if they didn't let themselves get lost in a forest of complacent indigence, they might be able to spot little islands of hope. The signal will be weak, but it will state, "I want to get up and get out more than I want to stay put." You have decided that you are one of those jewels that is willing to go to any lengths to reach that honorable first plateau of "working poor." Finding these fertile seeds is an acquired skill. Don't expect a job counselor to single you out for special treatment.

About fifteen years ago I took a ride with an attorney friend who was serving subpoenas on witnesses to an accident. This quest led us to a house barely hanging to the side of a steep hill in a section of town that had given up. There were no windows; indeed, there were no window frames, as they had long since been removed and sold. When winter came, I presumed they would put up tar paper or corrugated paper-board. The subject of the subpoena walked out when he saw our car, and proudly invited us in. I apprehensively entered the dark room and immediately tripped over a truck crankshaft lying in the middle of the floor.

As my eyes became accustomed to the dim room, I made out four young people of various sizes, all eating hot dogs and beans from paper plates while watching a game show on a small black and white TV. Springs protruded from the sofa, and soiled paper plates from past meals were scattered about. A tired woman, perspiring in a soiled slip, came into the room and served another paper plate to another silent child, paying no attention to us.

No one spoke, except the young man. He proudly and loudly spoke of worldly things, like subpoenas, court, and testimony. We left, shading our eyes from the bright sun. As we drove away in relief, my astute friend asked if I had noticed anything interesting about that encounter. I had noticed many things, but they were more pitiful than interesting.

"That girl. Did you see the girl? She was about sixteen, had on a clean dress, and her hair was tied in a ribbon." No, none of the denizens of the hovel we had just left fit that description. "That's because she split as soon as we drove up. She saw our car and bolted out the side door. She was standing by a tree across the road. She was ashamed, and who can blame her?"

I couldn't get that girl off my mind the rest of the day. My friend had seen shame. I had seen hope. Everyone else in that pigsty had accepted their lot as normal. They were probably better off than some of their acquaintances. They were eating, and they had a television. They even had a truck crankshaft, and maybe someday they would find a truck it would fit.

I shared this experience with a counselor at the Job Service. She was acquainted with the family, having contacted them when she was a county social worker. She knew the girl. Her name was Naomi, and she had seemed, well, different. That was the counselor's only recollection. Now, everyone in our line of work has an occasional Pygmalion fantasy in which we become the benefactor of some less fortunate soul. It usually involves inheriting a fortune, and then buying the grateful wretch out of a squalid condition. The counselor and I joked about this and decided our combined worth would barely buy her a bus ticket out of town.

Then, on a serious note, we wondered if Naomi's unconscious signal of dissatisfaction *really* meant that she might have that spark of life that cried out for priority time and attention. Her family was complacently existing in the third tent. Was she willing to forego the shepherding and provision of minimum needs by social agencies, and to surrender her total liberty from responsibility so as to get out and get over? The counselor and I decided to work out a plan to throw Naomi a lifeline.

What follows in the remainder of this book is an outline of a plan that resulted in Naomi's metamorphosis, written as a composite of many case studies of many counselees coming from similar situations. You know that Naomi did get out and get over and did become a happy and productive member of society, or I wouldn't be telling her story. Her good humor and acceptance of her quest as a team effort brought her successfully through the obstacle course. What we learned from her and her valiant and progressively successful successors was passed on to other counselors, to other vocational virgins, and now to you.

MAKING A DIFFERENCE: A WORD TO COUNSELORS

But first, a word to the counselor: While this book is addressed to the recovered alcoholic job seeker and other imperfect candidates for employment, our experience with previous editions has shown that it will be widely read by counselors. This little aside is for you counselors:

Once I helped with a scout troop in Washington, DC, and one of my many pleasurable tasks was to lead a patrol of boys on a nature walk in Rock Creek Park. One of my charges was a wide-eyed boy of eight—too young to be a full-fledged scout, but his big brother couldn't come unless he brought Harold along. Harold had never been far from the axis that connected his shabby apartment and school, and this excursion was like a trip through the looking glass. He asked questions about every tree, flower, bird, rock and squirrel.

One boy spotted a tiny green tree frog clinging to the bark of a birch sapling. I carefully picked it off, and allowed the boys to handle it while I discussed its feeding habits and protective coloration. When the frog came to Harold, he put his hands behind his back saying, "You touch a frog you get warts."

I saw this as a grand opportunity to correct a myth with hard scientific fact. I pedantically explained to Harold that people arrived at this mistaken idea because the skin of the frog had the appearance of little warts, adding that this was a method of camouflage to make him blend in with the tree's bark and protect him from his enemies. I then offered the frog to Harold a second time, and he backed off, declaring in a firm voice, "Touch a frog and you get *warts*, because *Momma says!*"

Assistant scout masters and counselors learn early: Don't mess with Momma.

There is always a strong temptation to counsel a vocational virgin as if you were a sculptor. But the men and women whom you will identify as willing candidates for this first transitional step from poverty to working poor are not lumps of clay. They have a strength of character that has cried out to you from the third tent: "I don't belong here!" With this character comes a well-developed personality that includes some biases, allegiances, and apocryphal knowledge that you will be tempted to tamper with. Unless these feelings and beliefs have an overwhelmingly adverse effect on the client's progress and job search, please learn to pass them by: "Don't mess with Momma."

So, you think you have spotted a strong heart and venturous spirit standing out among the mortally wounded casualties in the third tent. You have offered to help guide this salvageable human out through the obstacle course of poverty to a free and productive life. This requires getting a job, and getting a job requires changes. Remember that you are dealing with a willing subject you have spotted; *this is not an exercise in motivation.*

You have already made peace with the fact that you cannot save the world. You have the tools, you have a willing candidate, and you are going to make a difference in your little part of the universe. Let's go to work.

11

THE FIRST CHANGES

You're asked why you want to change, and you answer, "Because I want to be somebody."

Well, John D. Rockefeller was *somebody*, so was Martin Luther King, Jr. Jack the Ripper was *somebody*, as was St. Paul and Charles Manson. So what you really want is to be *somebody else*. You've looked around and decided there must be a better way, a better life. You're right about that, you know. But you still haven't answered the question, "Why?"

There are many reasons a person wants to change his or her life around. Some have religious reasons. Other folks don't really want to change their life around, they just want to feel better. They want more creature comforts. Would you be happy if everything stayed just like it is now, except somebody slipped two hundred in your pocket every week?

How about impressing others? If the good fairy pulled you out of your present condition and put you a thousand miles away with a good job, a nice car, and a fine wardrobe, would your first act be to shoot back to your old stomping grounds at the corner of Dirty Avenue and Ugly Street so you could tool back and forth with the top down and show off in front of your old acquaintances?

Many of your friends and possibly family members are willing to accept things the way they are. They may not like the way things are for them, but they are going to wait it out. One vocational virgin we worked with said she intended to ". . . just sit here until something good happens." "Something good," of course, meant hitting the number or finding a fat wallet.

You are *not* willing to sit there and wait, because you don't like what you are now, what you do now, how you look now, how you talk now, where you live now, and how you feel now. You want to do things that you can't do now, go places you can't go now, mingle with people you can't even approach now, talk about things besides sex and the weather, work at a job like real people, and be free to make exciting plans, not just dreams.

Listen to this theme written by a twenty-year-old woman in an adult GED preparation class. Only the spelling has been corrected.

> *What's going to become of me? Every day's like the day before. Same noise, same smells, same faces, same mess. I walk out into the street and see the same people doing the same thing——nothing. Same phoney rapping. Same bullshit about getting over and breaking out. But no matter what I say or do, everything will go on and on and stay just like it is—— miserable and boring. You ask what's going to become of me? Nothing, that's what.*

No, that's not what. Something is surely going to become of you. When I show friends a group picture taken when I was in the service years ago, I am dumbfounded that they wrongly identify someone else as me. I had no intention of changing that much, but it happened. You're going to change, too, whether you like it or not. You're going someplace.

We used to sing a gospel song, "This Train is Bound for Glory." I don't know if your train is bound for "Glory" or not, but it's surely going somewhere. It can't stand still. And you'd better decide that *you're* going to be the engineer. Because if someone else drives your train and pushes your buttons, you may find yourself on a trip you don't like and end up in a place you don't want to be.

You are about to start on a journey that will be bumpy in some spots and muddy in others. It will frequently be tiresome, because this will be a long trip with no rest stops. It may even be a little dangerous, as people around you may consider this awakening person to be a threat. And it will be a lonely trip, because you can't take along any passengers.

An early lesson you must learn is that *the only person you can change is yourself.* Legend has it that vampires hate mirrors because they don't show a reflection. In the original Dracula story, however, a character said that the mirror only reminded Count Dracula of what he was, and what he really hated was not mirrors, but himself.

You have to start liking yourself before you start on this journey. You are really worth the effort, or you wouldn't have come as far as the starting gate. You are already special.

NEED FOR SECRECY

You will start getting rid of excess baggage now, but most of it will be left behind as the trip progresses. There are many things you will not, or cannot, use once you reach your destination: old ideas, old habits, old fears, old resentments, and even a few old friends. There will be no big farewell party when you take off. No one except you will know you've left. You'll slip out and on your way "like a thief in the night."

The reason for all the secrecy is three-fold.

(1) If you grandly announce that you are planning to upgrade every aspect of your life, and if you survive the inevitable initial teasing, you will find you have saddled yourself with a large group of self-appointed critics. Every little mistake and course correction will be pointed out and thrown up to you. When others notice changes in your habits and style, you should either appear surprised and pass it off, or let them take some credit.

(2) If you "go public," you will unconsciously project an image of trying to be "better" than your friends and family, and that you are being critical of them for not coming up to your new standards. You may even be a threat to them; to their chosen lifestyle. Other people have their own baggage, their own map, and they're driving their own train.

(3) Broadcasting your trip can be very cruel, because you can't take anyone with you. Others may follow on their own, but you are the only passenger on this train.

There's the whistle. You can feel movement. It's already started. You've made the decision to change; quietly, completely, from the inside out.

WHAT YOU CAN CHANGE

You have the power to change only your own space, your own body, and your own mind.

But even these few potentials have limitations. You can't change your race or your height or your age. A few people have tried to cope with their dissatisfactions by surgically changing their sex, and others have dealt with an unacceptable home life by running away and living on the streets. But experience has shown that those solutions usually serve only to change problems into troubles. Let's start with things you can change: space, body, and mind.

Your Space

Your first reaction may be that this can't apply to you. If you live in a crowded apartment or a welfare dormitory, nothing—absolutely nothing—is private. "How can I change space that really isn't mine?"

Let's begin by taking charge of your own space. A high school English Composition class was given the assignment of writing a descriptive narrative on the subject, "A Visit to My Friend's House." Here was one offering:

I hate to go over to my friend's place. They live like pigs. There are newspapers and clothes all over, and the bathroom's cluttered with old toothpaste tubes and empty shaving stuff and the toilet's got icky stains and it stinks. I don't know what the bedroom looks like, because they keep the door closed. The radio and TV are always blaring away at the same time and you can't hear yourself think. There's always sticky stuff on the door knobs and linoleum floor and everything smells like dirty ash trays, beer, cabbage, and dog pee.

Try this on yourself. In your mind's eye, see if you can drift away from your body, and pretend to be approaching the place where you live as if you were a stranger. You have never been here before.

- What do you see?
- Hear?
- Smell?
- Feel?

Isn't it funny how we notice things about other people or other places that could very well apply to our own space? We get so used to seeing a crooked picture on the wall; stepping over our little sister's toy that's been in the middle of the floor for weeks; making breakfast around a pile of last night's (or last week's) dishes; sleeping in an unmade bed; using a dirty bathroom; getting dressed by fishing clothes out of a pile in the closet. It all seems normal so we blot it out. We work or play around these things and our mind makes them all disappear. But a visitor coming over would pick up on all that mess; that's how they would remember your place.

Your Bed

Now, close your eyes and picture yourself sitting on your bed. You look around. What do you see? What would a stranger notice? Hear? Smell? Does it feel like poverty? This is the beginning of the Yellow Brick Road.

You will start with the bed. This is *your* space; something you can change. It doesn't matter if it's a cot or a double bed or if you sleep alone or share the bed with one or three other people.

If you have sheets and a pillow case and they're dirty, you will wash them. Whether that's your job or not, you will wash them. Then you will make the bed, carefully and completely. If this is someone else's job, and they do it perfectly *every* morning, fine. Otherwise, you will make the bed, and you will do it without uttering a complaint or asking for praise.

If you are questioned about this unusual activity, you will simply say that you like it better that way.

Your Room

Now you're standing beside the bed; not as yourself, but as a stranger. How would you write the high school English report on "A Visit to My Friend's House"? What is lying on the floor? On the table? On the chair?

If you see old candy wrappers, dirty ash trays, newspapers, bottles, and dirty dishes, pick them up. "What if they're not mine?" *Pick them up!* Everything you see is part of your space and subject to your change. No arguments, no big deal and playing the martyr. Clothes get hung up. Everyone's clothes.

Absolutely no dramatics here. If there is anything that grates on the nerves it's a newly reformed slob preaching tidiness.

Each day from now on, you will look at your space again as a stranger, and you will gradually pick up on more little changes that will make the hours you spend there more peaceful.

The Bathroom

A bathroom is usually shared, but while you are using it, it is your space.

You scrub the sink, the mirror, and the toilet bowl. Yes, *and* the toilet bowl! If all of this is someone else's job, and they do it to perfection *every* day——fine. Otherwise, you do it. As you walk through the house, you will automatically and casually pick up and put away everything that is out of place. No more will you step over little sister's toy or big brother's beer bottle as if they were cracks in the sidewalk.

Storage Areas

Regularly and routinely inspect your wallet, purse, or briefcase. They will be cleaned out and placed in order.

If there is a dresser or desk drawer that is acknowledged as yours or one you share, it, too, will be subjected to regular purging and organization.

Most individuals and families have what they call a "junk drawer" that becomes the catch-all for everything that is on its way somewhere or doesn't have a place. Your possessions must be pulled out of this chaotic receptacle and either thrown away or put with your own things.

Throw away unneeded junk with courage and fortitude.

Your Building

Baltimore is a fine, progressive city that has made great strides in the past few years but, like every other large metropolis, it has its share of depressed neighborhoods. For the purposes of your own renewal project, note the difference between "poor" neighborhoods and "poverty" neighborhoods. A little over ten years ago, when unemployment was in double-digits all over the country and extremely high in inner cities, there were areas of Baltimore's poorer sections that stood out from the rest.

A section of town populated primarily by descendants of Eastern European immigrants was always immaculate. The sidewalks and front steps were scrubbed each morning and flowers bloomed in window boxes. And across town, driving through a very depressed area, you would be surprised by a banner stretched across the street that read, "Afro Clean Block." Neighborhoods displaying this proud banner had banded together in determination that being poor didn't mean living in a slum. They painted their doors and window sills, planted flowers in pots along the curb, and there was an unwritten rule that nobody could "hang out" on the sidewalk without holding a broom.

These people shared many things with their fellow poor Baltimoreans. They were nearly all on welfare. They all lived in tenement apartment buildings owned by heartless corporations that couldn't care less about their upkeep or appearance. But the one thing they refused to copy was an attitude of hopeless poverty.

When you leave your building, look back with a critical eye. If there is trash or litter around the front and you have automatically stepped over or around it for years, now you must pick it up. No matter if it isn't your bottle, or your empty cigarette pack, or your old newspaper. It is your space. No matter if the culprits will just throw down the stuff again tomorrow. You pick it up again tomorrow.

No hassle. No faultfinding. No big show of being the goody-two-shoes martyr. You just quietly pick up the trash, preferably when no one is around. You do this for the same reason you take a bath. It's a personal thing.

Noise

And now, a word about noise pollution. Even before a stranger picks up on the smells of a house or apartment, he or she will be aware of ambient noise. This is a sneaky type of pollution, because it not only dulls everyone's hearing, but forces them to talk louder —creating even more noise.

Since you've made the decision to take this trip up and out, you are too intelligent and survival prone to go around shutting off other people's TV programs, radios, and "boom boxes."

But you must not voluntarily duplicate distractions you are forcibly exposed to. While you may have no control over much of the radio or TV noise in your space, you can refrain from automatically turning on this background bedlam whenever you enter an empty room.

Also, a polite, "Anybody watching this TV? Do you mind if I turn it off?" can be prudently tested.

Many students think they can study better if they have the radio or stereo on or a Walkman headset glued to their ears. This isn't true. Starting over will frequently entail studying for a GED, a civil service test, a computer class, or even a driver's license. Trying to study in noisy surroundings is like hauling water in a leaky bucket. If the background noise cannot be controlled, you should go to the library.

While we're on the subject, "studying with somebody" (the favorite vehicle for getting out of the house as a teenager) always works best when that "somebody" is: (1) intelligent, (2) highly motivated, (3) has good study habits, (4) ambitious, (5) the same sex.

Most people who are forced to live in a loud environment learn to cope by developing shrill, screeching voices to talk through the din. You must learn to adjust your voice to meet the needs of the moment. You want the person you are speaking to to hear and understand you. That and no more.

Developing these good habits will carry over into your first job. You will be spending at least a third of your day there, and for that time, the work place is *your* space and *your* responsibility. This means that the same disciplined picking up, straightening, and cleaning you developed with respect to your home space applies equally to your work locker, the employees' room and, sometimes, to the restroom at work. You don't live like a slob anymore, and you don't have to work like a slob. The working day is a big chunk of your life. You deserve to make it livable.

BODY CARE AND APPEARANCE

Body care and appearance are already under your control.

Here is an area where you really start showing humility and self-discipline. You will be facing years of habit and strong peer pressure. Cultural and family acceptance of certain practices may be posing unnecessary obstacles to your trip over and out of poverty. Your friends and role models have established boundaries that form, for them, a permissible, ordinary "look." Experience has taught successful job counselors that this image may be far afield from an employer's acceptable limits of appearance and behavior.

Some of you may be too close to yourselves and your ideas of what is normal and acceptable in the job market to make an honest observation. You may need an outside opinion to identify what items of appearance and behavior are crying out for change. As you know, we have a tendency to believe that what *we* do is normal, what *they* do is weird.

And remember, we are not discussing what is right and what is wrong. There is nothing wrong with scuba diving gear—unless you happen to show up with tank, mask, and fins for a basketball game. Working up a sweat on the basketball court feels great, cleans out the pores, and is good all around—unless you are on your way to a job interview.

Any discussion of personal habits coming from a counselor presumes a high degree of mutual trust and respect between counselor and counselee. Furthermore, a counselor must try to dispense useful information while avoiding the cruelty of appearing judgmental and superior. That's why it is so much easier to discuss these things in a book. Maybe we're talking about you, then again, maybe we're not. Nevertheless, any changes will be made by *you* because:

- You made a decision to change, and to go to any lengths to reach certain goals.
- Through training, experience, and perseverance, you are learning how to reach those goals.
- The social rules you learn to comply with on the way up may seem dumb or confining, but they are merely bases we all must touch on the way to the goal.

The suggestions outlined in this and succeeding chapters are intentionally abbreviated and generalized so that you may tailor them to your own needs.

Drugs and Alcohol

As I've said before, sobriety is an absolute "must" of a serious job search. I won't dwell on the pitfalls of alcohol and drug abuse, as this is not a book on how to get straight. But if you think you are a candidate for vocational recovery and are still drinking or drugging, you're in for a wasted year and a queen-sized heartbreak. Your whole object is to change the odds in your favor so you can compete with "Mr. or Ms. Clean" in the job market.

Look at what happens to the odds when your attention is still focused on alcohol or dope.

- It consumes time, which you don't have.
- It consumes money, which you don't have.
- It consumes health, which you can't spare.
- It removes personal control that you are just starting to regain.
- It attracts "friends" who take and hurt.
- It repels friends who want to give and help.
- It replaces ambition with daydreams.
- It changes your odds from good to nonexistent.

Personal Hygiene

An early sign of addiction or depression is a lack of attention to cleanliness of body and dress. "Mr. Clean and Ms. Clean" have the advantage of having learned their personal hygiene habits at a parent's knee; or, they may also have had these traits finely honed in the military service. Counselors and other well-meaning folks have difficulty in tactfully suggesting needed corrective measures to an adult, so the subject is usually avoided. Don't skip any of the following paragraphs *even if you decide at first glance they don't apply to you!*

Here are some major points affecting successful job search that you may not have learned at a parent or drill sergeant's knee:

A clean body requires daily bathing. All over! Body odor really is offensive. Only in very exaggerated situations can one smell their own breath, body, and foot odor. These smells are mentally sorted out from a person's own senses just as the ever-present clutter of a bedroom or the litter around the front steps is not noticed when seen every day. Walking back through your memory, can you recall a friend, acquaintance, teacher, or co-worker who had bad breath or body odor? Isn't it true that *every time* you think of that person, like right now, that unpleasant sensory recall overwhelms all the other remembrances?

During a job search, the impression left by offensive breath or body odors can wipe out all of your positive moves.

Hair. Despite advertising hype, the best way to control dandruff is through frequent shampooing. If you have even a minor dandruff problem, be conscious of the fact that other people, especially those you are trying to impress (such as an employment interviewer), are aware of your problem, too. Like bad breath, dandruff has the power to fix a person's attention during a short meeting. At a reunion a few years ago, several old comrades and I had occasion to reminisce about a famous general we had served under. Instead of recounting the gallant and historic accomplishments of this honored man, we all talked about the distracting sight of dandruff forever salting his uniform shoulders and stars. So it will be with the job interviewer.

Beards and Mustaches. Beards and mustaches get dandruff, too, and when they do, they are absolutely fatal to a job interview. In fact, be wary of all mustaches and beards. They *do* change the odds. Mustaches have been the subject of many studies. People will more often associate a mustached stranger with distrust. I once participated in a project with a large group of personnel officers and managers. They were shown over a hundred photographs and were asked to guess, by looking at the eyes, which individuals had been caught stealing from their employers. The pictures were actually randomly selected from photo IDs of a state agency. Mustaches came in first; beards second.

If you decide to wear a mustache, you must carefully and regularly trim it. Absolutely no "walrus" hair hanging over the upper lip. It must be mature——not a few scraggly whiskers just sprouting. Adverse employer reaction seems strongest regarding mustaches on young applicants——twenty and below. African-American applicants are the exception to this subconscious bias.

No matter how well groomed, beards *always* divert an interviewer's attention away from the person and what he is saying. After a very short interview, only the beard is remembered.

Smoking

Smoking should be treated as another goal obstacle. The mistake of smoking during a job interview is covered in chapter 7. Whatever your personal feelings on smoking, it is important that you understand the current attitude regarding that addiction.

It is very possible that you do not know *anyone* who does not smoke. Nevertheless, the society and working world you are attempting to enter is moving in the direction of a smokefree twenty-first century.

Already all government buildings and most major corporations permit smoking only during authorized breaks and then only in specially designated areas. It is pitiful to walk past white-collar workers sitting on little chairs in the hallway "designated smoking areas." They are holding down important and responsible jobs, but here they are, on embarrassing public display, furiously inhaling their fix before their break is over.

More industries are including the term "nonsmoker" as a *bona fide* occupational requirement, and although some affected workers have taken this concept to court, most judgments are going against the plaintiffs. The reasons are easily understood by juries. In industries with a high degree of inhalant risk——for example fire departments, chemical or plastics plants——there is a high incidence of Workers' Compensation payments for lung and heart disabilities. The industries and their insurance carriers argue that they should not be liable for compensation to workers who intentionally damage their hearts and lungs off the job.

Please don't look upon this as a preachy antismoking message. It is merely routine job counseling. Believe me, the matter of smoking receives much attention at personnel and hiring conferences!

Avoid smoking during counseling meetings, including group sessions and visits to the Job Service. This is simply a realistic preparation for the world of work. It is a myth that people can relax and think better while smoking. The only thing a cigarette relaxes is the momentary craving for a cigarette. The fishing out, tapping, and lighting-up ritual is disturbing to the train of thought and distracting to others in the room. Calculate the actual cost of your habit in money, and decide from where in your budget the money comes. Clothes? Debt reduction? Transportation? Training manuals?

Accurate Sexual Information

Vocational counseling involves sexual guidance! Sexual hangups, attitudes, and misinformation have much to do with job preparation, job search, job performance, and job enjoyment.

The necessity of accurate sexual information and healthy sexual attitudes among women has an obvious vocational relationship and will be addressed first. Pregnancy, abortion decisions, day-care requirements, abuse by a mate, and disease exposure are only a few of the considerations that can concentrate a female job seeker's mind at the expense of a vigorous job search. Assure yourself that you have had or will have competent and professional advice on all aspects of sexuality. Instruction from family members and other "curbstone" experts doesn't count. Avoid going to individuals, groups, or organizations whose *primary* function is abortion referral. Sexual guidance is a much more comprehensive need than that represented by a narrow focus on birth control or pregnancy termination. Abstinence should be included as an option during this period of redirection and reorientation.

With few exceptions, men we have counseled were convinced they were born "cool" on matters of sex. The need for men to assess their real sexual comprehension and attitudes is particularly important. Young (and many not-so-young) men especially accept misinformation from peers, macho magazines, and other sources, and they find it agonizing to ask basic questions, admitting they are not all-knowing in this area. Responsibility and self-worth are absolute musts for long-term redirection and positive change. This entails:

- getting accurate information;
- being accountable for your part in making a baby;
- always considering your partner's best interests;
- taking responsibility for birth control;
- being alert to all health considerations; and,
- looking beyond the moment. (Are your present actions and attitudes compatible with your new goals? Or are they careless? Shortsighted? Selfish? Cruel?)

Sleep Habits

Going to bed and getting up are not routine habits for people who have been unemployed for years or have never worked at a regular job. You must determine how much sleep you need—not what you can get by with. You won't be taking afternoon naps and goofing off on a street corner. Make an honest estimate of when you must get up in time to get yourself cleaned up, dressed, fed, and to work once you get a job. Count backwards to arrive at a time you must start going to bed. Begin going to bed at that hour. That means *now*. Revising well-developed sleep habits after you get a job is much too late! This goes for Saturdays and Sundays, too. Sleeping late on these "free days" steals quality time and sets you up for a "blue Monday" once you start to work. (Time control will be covered in more detail later in this chapter.)

Exercise and Diet

Walking when the practical possibility exists is a very inexpensive method of clearing the mind and saving a buck. Add stair climbing and you have a beautiful replacement for books on "Power

Walking" and aerobic video tapes. This does not include racing to a job interview only to arrive looking and smelling like a wet billy goat.

Logically, one would expect a poor person to spend much less on food than someone who has a comfortable income. During the Great Depression of the 1930s, large families were raised on a cheap but healthy diet composed almost exclusively of beans, greens, corn bread, and skim milk. The young adults I have counseled in recent years who come from poor families seem to be surviving on a menu of soda, barbecued potato chips, and pizza. Not only is this a dangerous diet from the standpoint of sodium, cholesterol, and low nutrition, but it is terribly expensive.

Always have breakfast. You'll pay for a regular regimen of bacon, eggs, and buttered grits with a heart attack at age fifty. But you should force-feed yourself *something* before you start your daily job search. This can be an apple, glass of juice or milk, or a bowl of "grown up" type cereal. A cup of coffee and a cigarette do not count.

Be prepared for a "quick fix." When you are hungry——whether it is nervous hunger or an actual empty belly——anything will do. When we are hungry, our minds fantasize about food, and the smell of a hamburger joint may drive us to an off-schedule meal. This is also the point where alcoholics will be told by their subconscious mind to put down the hunger with a drink. Carrots, an apple, crackers, will all do the trick. I make it a habit to keep a few Rye Crisp crackers in my brief case. It serves as a "quick fix," and my mind is instantly off food or drink and back to the business at hand.

When you are venturing forth on your first job, please be wary of co-workers with bad lunch routines. I always advise my clients to "brown bag" for a minimum of six months. Once you've accepted a few invitations from new friends to join them for a lunch that turns out to be a "greasy spoon special," or lasagna and beer, or maybe just beer, it's hard to break out of the ritual. You also may find it hard to get back to work.

CLOTHING AND STYLE

The uniform a person wears makes an indelible impression.

Consciously or not, most people wear their clothes, hair, make-up, and jewelry to make a public statement. Many of us deny this, saying that we only dress for ourselves. This, of course, is usually untrue, unless one happens to be a deep-sea diver or space walker. Some of us leave the house wearing a get-up that says, "I'm a free spirit, and I don't care what people think of me. I'll dress any damn way I please." That of course is just another statement; one that is usually understood by all contacts.

Television time is expensive, and the average viewer's attention span is short. For that reason, TV writers take advantage of uniform stereotypes to convey instant character descriptions. Visualize a big city detective, a mugger, a fundamentalist preacher, a mobster, a prostitute, a child molester, or a female business executive. No problem; one or two images immediately flash on your mental screen.

For decades we have been warned by sociologists to beware of forming generalizations based on stereotypes, and counselors-in-training are especially cautioned against that defect. In simple terms, "generalizing" just means jumping to conclusions about somebody because of past experiences. If a bald-headed man ran over your motorcycle, you might be tempted to conclude that all bald-headed men were dumb drivers. That would be a stereotype generalization.

But if our contact with an individual is limited to a short experience, we will form an opinion, and it *will* come from what we observe plus our previous experience and hearsay. It will be stereotypical. For example, if two people walk into a bank wearing ski masks and carrying black satchels, they may intend to deposit their pay checks before running off to Aspen for the weekend. The bank guard who blows them away may have made a stereotypical generalization.

It is no sin to dress in a way that makes you feel comfortable and lets you melt in with your current crowd. But we have learned from accurate research and intimate experience that the best way to achieve initial acceptance in the working world is through compliance with the comfortable norm. That means a norm that is comfortable to the employer, not necessarily to you or your current friends. The *Appearance Advantage* is discussed in chapter 1, and should be reviewed for specific pre-job search guidance. The items listed below are for general discussion on this subject.

When making a decision about your appearance in your job search, your standard should be this statement: "I want you to want to hire me more than you want to hire someone else."

Learn to Recognize the Norms

Start by observing what employers wear to work every day. Take a critical look at yourself *from an employer's standpoint.* How many of your dress habits (including hair style and jewelry) have you copied from entertainers you admire or losers you hang out with? People in the entertainment business—such as Mr."T" or Madonna—have a reason for outrageous appearance. It is a uniform of their work, just as welders and scuba divers wear special clothes. Unlike you, these people are not looking for work with little experience and no references.

"Sorry, we're not hiring bizarre today." You can admire someone without copying styles of dress and other adornments. Gregory Hines wears an earring. Hines has been dancing and acting for decades and has earned a position at the top of his profession. But many years ago when he was on his way up to the top, he appeared regularly on the Ed Sullivan TV show with *Hines, Hines, and Dad.* Gregory Hines was smart enough to dress in a way that didn't offend Ol' Ed.

Malcolm-Jamal Warner wears an earring and a pigtail. He plays a rich college kid on the Bill Cosby Show, but you can bet he didn't wear earrings and a pigtail when he first auditioned for the part!

Howard Hesseman, who used to play an alcoholic ex-hippie on "WKRP Cincinnati," recently played a teacher on the show "Head of the Class." The producers and writers decided that his character should wear a pony tail. In real life, suppose a school board were faced with two equally qualified male applicants and one of them wore a pony tail. How much of your own money would you bet on the pony tail getting the job? And remember, in your job search, you won't even be equally qualified in the eyes of the employer, because your competition, "Mr. Clean," will have job experience and good references.

The Kennedy brothers were the idols of long-haired, bearded, "liberated" youth in the 1960s. But the Kennedys were no dummies. They were looking for work (the Presidency), so they shaved, bathed, and cut their hair.

Identify the Middle Ground. You don't want to have the "white sidewalls" look of a 1940s movie; nor do you want to be remembered as the person with the freaked-out mop. *"Be not the first by whom the new is tried, nor last to lay the old aside."* (From Shakespeare's *Hamlet*)

All tattoos that can possibly be covered will be placed out of sight during all job interviews.

Female job seekers are cautioned to refrain from appearing for job interviews with hair styles, make-up, dresses, and shoes more appropriate for evening disco wear. False eyelashes, heavy eye shadow, excessive rouge, "punk" hair styles, and miniskirts all may look cute and sexy on the dance floor, but can be dreadful in the broad daylight. Employers simply will not take an applicant in such a costume seriously. Furthermore, sofas and chairs in waiting rooms frequently tilt the sitter at an angle distressing to the wearer of a very short skirt.

Any perfume must be very subtle. It is no substitute for soap and deodorants. Put your green, black, purple and silver nail polishes on hold. And no gum!

Shoes will be clean or shined, and appropriate to the job interview. Employers are still too square to appreciate the utility of sneakers with a suit jacket. Hundred-dollar Reeboks may make a hit on the street corner, but if you are looking for an office or sales job or any position with a chance for advancement, an employer will wonder why a grown-up is wearing gym shoes to a job interview.

All clothes will be clean; especially shirts. Light-colored shirts and blouses simply will not bear multiple wearings between washes.

Fingernails must be trimmed and clean.

The evaluation begins in the waiting room; not at the interview desk. Most receptionists are skilled observers whose judgment is respected by employers. It doesn't matter how cool you are during an interview if you behave boorishly in the outer office. You should always act as if you were being watched by a hidden camera. (This indeed might be the case. I have also known employers to place a member of their staff in the waiting room posing as another applicant.)

TIME MANAGEMENT

"Dost thou love life? Then do not squander time, for that's the stuff life is made of." (Benjamin Franklin, 1741). True then; true now. And doubly true for the vocational virgin who is trying to play catch-up with the rest of the world.

Individuals or families finding themselves staring bankruptcy in the eye may seek the services of a financial counselor. The first exercise they will be told to do will be to keep a brutally honest and complete record of all expenditures—whether for a new car or a pack of gum. The very act of listing each item for which money is spent starts the process of financial maturity.

Your Time Budget

Time is similar to money: It can't be spent twice, and it is subject to wise and foolish investment. I am giving you the assignment of preparing a *time budget*, the first step being an honest, and embarrassingly complete listing of how time is spent in a given day. Time that is habitually paid out on unneeded or harmful activities is available to you to invest in career and life preparation. Your time, and how you invest it, is another thing that is under your control.

Early in your exercise of honestly recording time, you probably will see a heavy time allocation to the following categories:

- Radio, TV, and recordings
- Nonproductive rapping and gossip
- Daydreams and sexual fantasies
- Smoking
- Repeated, unnecessary and wasteful trips to the same place due to poor planning
- Nervous eating.
- Junk reading
- Unearned catnaps
- Waiting for busses, appointments, tardy friends
- Gaps of time wasted due to unexpected cancellations

You'll notice that drinking and drugging are not listed as available time. If you are still into either, the whole exercise is a waste of, yes, time.

You will soon discover that the mere act of listing activities and keeping track of time spent on each action will start the ball rolling toward change. You will want to repeat this little task every few weeks. Comparing current and old time inventories is a good way to see progress. It also will force you to stop insisting you didn't have time to do a much needed task connected with your job search.

You can't spend the same dollar twice, and you can't spend the same hour twice. As you work with your time investment portfolio, weave the following thoughts and corrective suggestions into your planning:

Learn the polite "No" response. Agreeing automatically to every suggestion another makes, simply because you cannot come up with an iron-clad excuse to say no, is a dangerous time waster and forfeiture of control.

Work an eight-hour day. This idea for recovered substance abusers is given its well-deserved full treatment in chapter 8. It is especially important for vocational virgins.

Do not take a break before a job is started. Breaks are earned, saved, and cashed in when needed.

Keep a small notebook. A little pocket-sized notebook and ballpoint pen are indispensable tools of anyone serious about their growth and job search. Specific tasks for the day will be jotted down as they come to mind. The next day a new list will be started with unfinished chores copied from the previous day. If a job has to be recopied day after day, it may suggest procrastination, or the possibility that the task should be dropped from the list. You will not become a slave to these lists. The purpose is not to turn you into a robot but to give you access to productive alternatives to unexpected down time. This idea is covered in more detail in chapter 8.

Recognize time as the precious commodity it is. Vilfredo Pareto, the nineteenth-century sociologist and economist, formulated the theory that in any large undertaking, eighty percent of the positive results are the product of only twenty percent of the effort. This means that most people spend eighty percent of their time and energy trying to accomplish that other little twenty percent. Sales managers have expanded this idea by showing that eighty percent of their total sales are to only twenty percent of their customers. This observation may help you identify areas where you are spending too much time, energy, and frustration on a task that isn't worth that investment.

For example: A new job holder spends all spare time and money trying to keep a beat-up car running, and it still breaks down frequently, making him late for work. Finally, he gets smart and sells the car for junk, paying a co-worker gas money for a regular ride. Money was systematically set aside for purchase of reliable transportation.

Another example: A young woman signed up for a nursing assistant course because her friend had registered. She had little aptitude and less interest in the field, but was determined not to give up or fail. She spent many precious evenings and weekends working toward a goal that would, at best, provide her with a fall-back occupation.

Eliminate the doing of things that may have to be undone later. Let your imagination run with this a bit. It includes everything from dropping your dirty clothes on the floor to making an enemy.

There is never a good excuse for being late. "Never" may be a bit strong, here. But it is a lead-pipe cinch that, from an employer's point of view, there is never an *acceptable* excuse for being late. I have reviewed thousands of employment interview notes, and a large percentage show whether the applicant arrived for the interview at the appointed time.

Bad weather? Only the Sahara has reliable weather. Plan to leave early.

Car trouble? Always have alternate public or other transportation planned and tested.

Baby sitter didn't show? Plan several alternates, friends, relatives, or use of a temporary day care, and move quickly into "Plan B" the moment the clock hits a predetermined fail-safe time.

Using the twenty-four-hour inventory. Many years ago, a counselor who was guiding me through some difficult times gave me a twenty-four-inch ruler. It was a yard stick he had snapped off at the twenty-four-inch mark. He instructed me to mount the ruler on the wall of my bedroom, where I could see it after I had gotten into bed for the night. Each inch represented an hour of the day I had just completed. At the six-inch line I had gotten up. I was at work at the eight, and so through the day until here I lay at the twenty-two-inch mark. As I moved my finger across the ruler, I took a walk through my memory. What would I change if I were given that day again? What minutes or hours of that priceless day had I misused? What had I foolishly done that would have to be undone tomorrow?

12

LANGUAGE

Language can be a dramatically vivid uniform of poverty.

How people use the English language stereotypes them as to intelligence, education, competence, sincerity, diligence, trainability, and potential much more than do the standard road signs of bigotry—race, sex, and physical features. This is a fact. It is not a sociological theory.

It is important not to confuse cultural dialects with regional accents. Appalachians who have had even a modest education or contacts outside their own hollow do not talk like *Snuffy Smith*. They are also quick to identify those who do as "hillbillies." Barbara Jordan has a Texas accent, but she speaks beautiful standard English, and she insists that her students do the same. People listen to Barbara Jordan.

A major national insurance company had agreed to hire several of our "classified-disadvantaged" applicants as summer clerical interns, with the opportunity to become permanent employees. We were delighted with this offer, because it gave us a chance to place a group of our vocational virgins in entry level positions.

All of the applicants we referred for these jobs had been tested for clerical aptitude and had been trained in basic office skills. I sat in on several interviews. One woman in particular seemed to have the interview nailed down. She had all the right answers, and her bright smile and obvious enthusiasm made her an apparent "shoo-in."

Then the interviewer asked, "Would you be comfortable filling in at the reception desk or switchboard?" The aspirant's response hit the interviewer like a bucket of cold water. "Oh, sure. I've already *did* that lots of times."

I could tell by the line of questioning that she was being considered for an interesting and responsible entry position, but this one answer put the interview on a different course, and she was sent to the typing pool. Fair or not, the interviewer talked with over twenty-five applicants that day, and he had to make his decisions based on eight- to ten-minute encounters. Just or unjust, on a job interview, the game is frequently "one strike and you're out."

USE STANDARD ENGLISH

Speech peer pressure is a powerful and cunning force. Job counselors are not immune to this failing, either. Those of us who condemn peer pressure loudest may be terrified to defy the current wisdom of our peer group.

But remember your goal! It is time to understand that your present role models are not necessarily right for you now.

Children who have heard only giggly baby talk from infancy through the first five years enter kindergarten with screwed up communication concepts. Do not let a counselor, minister, teacher, or Job Service interviewer talk *down* to you. If you sense that this is happening, let them know you are working to correct your grammar, and insist that they use standard English with you (provided they have that capability). Always use standard English with those contacts. Explain that this is an integral part of your job preparation. Invite teachers, counselors or other *qualified* support contacts to make corrections as they occur in your speech.

Begin switching to standard English in all conversation. However, sudden changes in your speech may attract unwelcome attention for several reasons: (1) This will blow your cover (review chap. 11); (2) An abrupt change will be interpreted by friends and enemies alike as pretentious or snobbish, and they may be right; (3) As soon as your friends and family suspect that you are trying to "better yourself," you may create an instant pool of critics eager to catch you in a real or imagined fluff.

Begin your change with a total elimination of swearing. I guarantee that no one will notice. This will force you to collect a ready reserve of suitable substitute words.

Listen to the speech of your friends and acquaintances with a critical ear. How would their language sound to a job interviewer? Unlike the simultaneous interpreters at the United Nations, few people can turn cultural speech habits on and off as the occasion demands.

Never correct someone else's English unless you are in an appropriate role (Big Sister or Brother, parent, fellow counselee).

Speaking standard English does not mean using big words. Make sure you know the proper pronunciation and meaning of new words and terms you pick. Using words that you *know* your listener does not understand is:

- Not honest communication
- The worst kind of snobbery
- A cruel put-down
- Unworthy of the person you are trying to become

There is also a possibility that a premature display of big, ill-fitting, pompous words also might be mispronounced, misused, and make you look a bit foolish.

On the other hand, there will be many new words that you hear others use, or that you begin to notice in books, the newspaper, or on TV newscasts. Do not hesitate to look them up, and work them into a conversation.

Understand that your language adjustment is vital to your mission. You are changing slowly——from the inside out. The use of standard English must be an early and continuous task.

READING

Reading improvement is directly related to other aspects of upward movement. Do you have any idea what your reading level is? Now is the time to find out—otherwise you won't have a baseline to use when you want to measure improvement. If you are reading this book on your own, and have managed to comprehend what is being said without *constant* use of a dictionary, you are reading at a high school level. People reading below that level have usually developed a talent for sliding over words they don't know without missing too much. You can watch the news on TV and not understand all the big words the announcer spits out, but still have a good idea of what shape the world's in. Adult job seekers usually do not have the time to take formal remedial reading classes, and unless you are having someone read this to you, you can improve your reading on your own.

Interest-Centered Reading

I suggest an alternative approach to reading improvement that we have used successfully for many years. When I come across a client whose reading skills are handicapping the trip up and out of poverty, I make reading assignments from tabloids and popular magazines and issue a pocket dictionary. An adult client who would balk at struggling through *Tom Sawyer* may enjoy spending evenings working with an article on Darrel Strawberry in *Sporting News*, or Madonna's latest exploits in the *National Enquirer*. The vocabularies of these publications are pitched at eighth grade or below, and they are a good starting point.

I once worked with a client who was fascinated with cars although he had never owned one. His total experience with automobiles was limited to bus rides and a few trips as an involuntary passenger in a police car. I selected an automotive magazine with a very modest vocabulary and marked an article for him to read. Since I am not a car buff, I first went over the story with a mechanically inclined colleague who explained the jargon, technical terms, and acronyms that were casually tossed about.

These I typed on a card with simple definitions, and inserted the card as a bookmark.

I never spent more than a few minutes of our counseling time discussing his reading assignment, but as his speed and comprehension improved, I gradually upgraded the material to automotive magazines targeted toward a more literate reader. My counselee always appeared with his magazine in his hip pocket, and the pocket dictionary was needed less and less.

As our rapport developed, he confided that he and his friends used to stand around and rap about the quality and performance characteristics of this car or that—mumbling words like "suspension" and "rack and pinion steering." He realized now that *nobody* in that crowd had any idea what they were talking about. He had looked up to those losers but now realized he was outgrowing them.

The Blessed Library

The public library is the answer to the serious job seeker's prayers. (Please refer to chapter 3.) Get a library card immediately. Call the library and ask about a convenient slow period when you can come in and get your card, along with a tour of the stacks and a description of the services. Ask about the location of books and magazines in your interest area.

Humbly inform the librarian that you are not familiar with the nuts and bolts of the library. You will want to know what is available, how to check books out, how to use the *Reader's Guide*, the index, the whole shootin' match.

Ask the librarian's name, and remember it. Calling someone by their name is both courteous and flattering. It will pay off in future service.

Select short books (200-250 pages) unless you are already an avid reader. This prevents discouragement. For the same reason, you should initially avoid checking out books on the best-seller list or other books on the "7-Day" shelf. These books usually cannot be renewed, and returning unfinished books is depressing.

If you have honestly determined that the book you selected was not what you thought, or is simply too difficult, you should exchange it immediately without plowing through it just to prove a point.

Get in the habit of returning your books on time. Don't start spinning excuses about a "five-day grace period" on overdue books, or the fact that the fine is only twenty-five cents, or that you ran three blocks from the bus and the library was closed. *Being late for anything, or with anything, for any reason is a broken promise and reinforces a habit that is totally unacceptable in the working world.*

Start the habit of always putting your library book in the same place. Lost books are expensive. Library patrons who lose books also tend to stop using the library out of fear and embarrassment.

Personal libraries are not only for the rich. Introduce yourself to the exciting world of LIBRARY SALES! These regular events are used to clear outdated and duplicated books from the shelves to make room for new items. Patrons of the public library also donate books, and many people designate the local library as recipient of their personal book collections upon death. Fully half my reference books have come from library sales, and some of my more valued and frequently used volumes were purchased for one dollar. They could not be replaced for twenty or thirty dollars.

If you take me up on attending library sales, let me caution you against picking up "bargain" novels. These are books you could check out at the public library. Reference books cannot be checked out. Those are the books you want to own!

You only have to learn a new word once. Keep a sheet of lined paper folded lengthwise as a bookmark. By writing down all the words you do not *fully* understand, you can look them up at the first opportunity and note a brief definition on your bookmark.

You will soon discover that most authors use the same unusual words repeatedly. Once you know the meaning and pronunciation, say these new words over *out loud* until they fall comfortably and gracefully off your tongue. By the time you have finished the book you will *own* those words, and they'll no longer be unusual!

Most employers presume that everyone has a basic knowledge of current events. Rightly or wrongly, many people associate awareness of the news with intelligence. To put the job applicant (or themselves) at ease, many employers will engage in a few moments of small talk, most probably about the weather or the front page of today's paper. If the governor of your state is involved in a sex scandal, and you don't know who the governor is, an immediate judgment will be made——incorrect or not——that you are generally stupid.

See if you can get a map of the world to put on your wall. For a few quarters, you can photocopy sections of a world map from an atlas at the library (ask the librarian——it will be in the reference section). Every time a country is mentioned on the news and you don't know exactly where it is and what its capital is, check it on your map.

Always be in the process of reading a book. If anyone pulls the classic cliché on you about, "Read any good books lately?" you ought to be able to say, "As a matter of fact, yes, I have!"

Gradually steer your reading into areas of your job interest and aptitude. This will come after you have completed the steps explained in Part I of this book. Initially, your idea of the variety of job opportunities available to you could be quite narrow. During this period, development of good reading habits alone may be enough of a challenge.

But later, as you learn that you don't have to be locked into anything, that the world did not just wake up one morning and decide it was going to hold you down, you can start heavy reading in the career of your choice. It is exciting to realize that you can know more about almost any subject——health care, automobile mechanics, agriculture, computers, airplanes, sales, cooking, and so on——than anyone else on the job. You can be the sharpest person in your field at the plant, office, or store. And all that information is right in your library and it doesn't cost a nickel.

WRITING

Writing may have to be relearned, like skating or diving. Many of you have not written much more than your name since you left school. Expressing yourself in writing does not come as a biological urge, like eating, breathing, or sex. Furthermore, if we don't do something well, we frequently become discouraged and quit.

Writer's block is not a mental illness confined to authors. Many people who are well-schooled in English freeze up when confronted with a blank piece of paper and a ticking clock.

However, if your career goals are still intact, you must develop your writing skills. Letters to prospective employers, interview notes, and thematic, or "story" questions on applications are just a few writing chores you will regularly and routinely face in your job search. And *after* being hired, the need for written communication will mushroom as you move up the career ladder.

Since most of you are not working or conducting your job search in institutional settings such as hospitals or prisons, where you can take free courses in English composition, consider the following suggestions. They are directly linked to your job search and the techniques outlined in Part I of this book. There is a practical job search application in each step, and it is also good fun.

Start a Diary

This will not be a fancy or expensive diary, made and sold for that purpose. It will be a small, pocket-sized, inexpensive, but sturdy notebook. Start with these entries:

Date and weather. Overcome the scariness of the blank page by routinely entering the date and a one- or two-word weather comment such as: "6/15/92; cold, windy." These are not optional entries. They will become very important reference points as your diary graduates into a job-search ledger. This also serves to personalize the page, keeping it from becoming just another bunch of hodgepodge entries.

Entries will be written in small, neat, straight lines. No one else needs to see this diary; it will not be graded. It may be the first totally private task you've done for a long time. Nevertheless, neatness *does* count. A hasty scrawl may provide an adequate memory jog for twelve or twenty-four hours, but not for future reference. How often have we said, "I can't read my own writing."? This is because the time limit on our short-term memory has expired. A carelessly written phone number may have 7s that could pass as 2s, and 8s that could well be 0s. Names and titles must be spelled out; preferably block printed.

Make entries short, but complete. Every name and phone number must be identified. Nothing is more exasperating for a serious job seeker (or any of us, for that matter) than to find a phone number on a scrap of paper or in a notebook with no identification. It must have been important, or it wouldn't have been written down in the first place. Could it be some personnel office that wanted you to check back in a few days? A good job lead you copied out of the paper? An appointment your counselor made for you?

And now a word about "lists." The division of opinion on list makers has become the subject of many foggy barroom arguments. The same people who declare that they are "dog people" or "cat people," and never the twain shall meet, also may think that everyone who makes lists is a nerd.

I have had many employees who were steadfast and hardheaded "nonlist" people. After several episodes of missed appointments, unreturned phone calls, and sloppy planning, I usually instructed them to obtain a notebook from the supply cabinet, and use it. Any counselor who does not have an appointment list and a work plan is either not a very busy counselor or not a very good counselor. Probably both.

List appointments and things to do. These items will be noted below the date and will be separated with an initial dash (-), not a number. Numbering lists prioritizes entries, and you are recording these things as you think of them.

Things not accomplished the day they are entered are copied the next day. It will be a fresh, new page (dated and with a note about the weather). A neat, single, diagonal line is drawn through the previous day's entries.

Any item that is recopied day after day is either being put off and should be done immediately or is not really important and might be dropped from the list. Some of the latter items might be transferred to a long-range plan in the back of your notebook. I have a special space in the back of my pocket notebook and also a directory in my computer I call "The Pantry." There I put ideas that I don't need right now, but might in the future. The notebook works for you; you do not work for the notebook!

Reserve the inside cover of your notebook, both front and back, for permanent storage of names, addresses, *identified* phone numbers, and good ideas. These should be written very neatly and as small as practical, due to limited space.

Date and store old notebooks. This is no big deal. Six months worth of notebooks secured with a rubber band will take less drawer space than your pocket dictionary. Rarely will your first few jobs become permanent, full-time employment. When you resume your job search, you will already have a ready reference of names, numbers, and comments of target employers you've previously considered. Many of those you tried might have hired you if they'd had an opening then. Permanent names, phone numbers, and other information should be copied from the inside covers of the old notebooks to the new.

Expand your writing activity. This will include notes on the day's job search—including the home runs, base hits, foul balls, strikeouts, and errors. It also will include updated target data (see chap. 6). Other possibilities for diary inclusion might be:

- A note about what book you are now working through
- Things you want to kick around with your counselor at the next session
- Income and expense log

Write Letters

The telephone has reduced letter writing to the point that it is nearly a lost art. This is unfortunate, because our telephone conversations rarely represent well-thought-out communication and therefore do not show our true feelings. Written transcriptions of telephone conversations that are introduced as trial evidence are always embarrassing to defendants. This is not only because of the incriminating content, but for the inane and seemingly endless drivel that passes as conversation when people talk on the phone.

Postcards. Postcards are an excellent vehicle for restarting a sleepy or virginal letter writing habit. They only cost a few cents. Their small size limits the message; no big, scary, blank sheet of paper. Four or five can be bought at a time before you really need them. This permits impulse writing—spontaneously—just for the hell of it! Write impulse postcards to:

- The Editor of the local paper
- TV news anchors
- Fan postcards to TV, movie, or sports favorites
- Store president: "I got some bad-smelling chicken from you last Saturday," or "Why don't you carry Thermos refills?"
- The mayor, the governor, your U.S. Representative, senator, the President of the United States
- The author of the book you've just plowed through
- Me! (care of the Publisher, whose address is in the front of the book).

You can get the addresses at the library, either from special directories that the librarian can show you or from the *World Almanac.* You will be pleasantly surprised to learn that all notes to these and other public figures will be answered—maybe not immediately, but they *will* be answered. Again, expand your writing to include notes to a relative, someone in service, even a pen pal picked up from your church's mission society. You may get someone to proofread your drafts for spelling and grammar if that makes you more comfortable at first. You are not getting into letter writing as a hobby or to improve your social graces. Communicating in writing is a process you must learn to be comfortable with to deal with the competition, Ms. and Mr. Clean.

13

NEW RELATIONSHIPS

New relationships may be a side effect (or bonus) of leaving the poverty mindset. If you have been careful about guiding yourself through this transformation, your drifting apart from old ties can be very gentle.

OLD FRIENDS

You should maintain the mystery of what is happening to you. Neither old friends nor new friends should know everything about your plans or aspirations. Dramatic separations should be avoided if possible.

- They are frequently ego trips.
- They are nonproductive, occupying your mind and squeezing out more creative work.
- They can make unnecessary enemies.
- They are often cruel.
- They could be dangerous.

NEW FRIENDS

You will be exposed to a different group of individuals and will attract many who will want to be your friend——some good, some bad.

There will be a time when you feel you are in a relationship vacuum. This happens to both men and women who are moving up and out. I saw one of our counselees on the street one day and commented that it was a pleasure to see her smiling for a change. She replied, laughing, "I guess I'm just in between enemies."

A few days later I saw her sitting alone on the steps of our office, an open book in her lap, just staring into space. She was starting to feel that she was also in between friends. It was not the case, but that was the way she perceived this passage in her life. This is because old acquaintances are always easy, like an old pair of shoes. But there is a good reason why people spend much time and effort growing flowers instead of weeds, although weeds are easy and require no commitment. During this interval between the old you and the new you, you will be especially vulnerable to predators, vultures, button pushers, and thirteenth steppers.

"Thirteenth Stepper" is a word that has become part of the unofficial jargon of Alcoholics Anonymous. There are, of course, only Twelve Steps in the AA recovery program. "Thirteenth Stepper" is a put-down term that refers to any member who takes sexual advantage of a sick, lonely, confused and trusting newcomer. A "bird dog," if you will. Substance abuse counselors who work in institutions that treat both men and women quickly learn to identify the studs and sexpots who keep a weather eye on the registration desk.

Beyond the opportunistic seducers, others will attempt to take you under their wing. They will be free with advice, but if they are losers themselves, you are already out of their league. These are the "button pushers," who have a great need to control people, place great demands on their time, and are patronizing with unasked-for counsel. Train yourself to recognize new acquaintances who are too eager to give you advice and guidance; whether about dress, companion selection, social activities, or job search. Losers love to share the secrets of their "success."

WINNERS AND LOSERS

Learn to spot them, and soon, before close relationships or entangling alliances develop. The winners will not necessarily be the most popular people in the crowd, since popularity is not their goal. If it happens, it happens. No big deal. But popular, outgoing people, whether they are winners or losers, are always easier to get to know. If those popular people also happen to be shallow losers, you may find yourself cultivating weeds.

That is why it is important to widen your world of choice. You can start by regularly speaking to all acquaintances and learning to pay people compliments without seeming oily and patronizing. Having many good friends with whom you do not have an exclusive attachment is a learned art.

You will learn to measure your old and new friends by their:

Humility

Winners in life recognize that they are not the center of the universe. Oh, they like themselves, all right. But humility does not mean thinking less of yourself. *It means thinking of yourself less.*

Honesty

A person's attitude toward honesty tells us much about their entire character. You do not have the time nor do you need the aggravation of having to decide whether every other sentence a companion utters is true. People who lie about the past will also lie about the future. Now we're talking about trust, the breaking of promises, the betrayal of confidences, and taking on an emotional burden that could threaten everything you have accomplished.

Respect

If you are hanging out with the winners, your new friends would: 1) never do or say anything to hurt you; 2) never ask you to hurt yourself or another person; and, 3) not gossip about others, showing that they probably will respect you too . . . when you're not around.

Sharing

A winner will not be jealous of: 1) sharing your friendship with others; 2) your taking a different scholastic, career, or interest path; 3) your asking for a second opinion when offered advice; or, 4) your relationship with your counselor or substance abuse program sponsor.

Enthusiasm for Life

Winners have a zest for living that translates into caring for their bodies through cleanliness, good diet, drug abstention, and preventive medicine; development of their minds, with a holy curiosity and hunger for truth and knowledge; and achieving, and not quitting.

LOVE

What in the world does this topic have to do with getting a job? I heard a World War II flight instructor lament that all his cadets either had tried to land with their wheels up or were going to try to land with their wheels up. I'd extend that to say all counselors have either had the following experience or will suffer through it too often in the future.

The counselor's intake people have spotted a good candidate for special, in-depth counseling. She is dissatisfied with her life, is willing to work hard and long, and is determined to change into a happy, joyous, free, and productive person. The first sessions with her convince the counselor she is a terrific contender for triage out of the third tent. She can really make it up and out of the poverty pit. Soon she begins taking charge of her space, her body, and her mind. Her language shows marked improvement, and she has started developing practical and exciting career goals.

One day she announces that a boyfriend has moved in with her. The counselor recognizes the name; he's a drugged-out bum.

This is heartbreaking for the counselor. Like the mythical Cassandra, the counselor can predict the future, but no one will believe her. That is why I am including this discussion in this book on job search. If it is appropriate to you, great. If not, file it away for future reference or for use with your children. I have to give this my best shot, because I've lost too many fine folks with real potential for getting out of the poverty pit because they followed a Pied Piper they thought was "love."

The Greeks had three words for "love": *eros*, *adelphos*, and *agape*. We try to make do with one. Before you try to define your version of "love," be aware of a few things that love is not.

Not a One-Way Infatuation

If you don't "love each other," it is simply lust. When I was a small boy, Shirley Temple was the darling of Hollywood. I fell head over heels in love with her. I was surprised, hurt, and angry when I learned that my buddy down the road felt the same passion for Shirley. This anger turned into jealous rage, and I defended Shirley's honor behind the barn, suffering a split lip and a torn shirt for my trouble. And Shirley never knew. A one-way adoration is no different than my crush on Shirley Temple. It doesn't matter if you're nine years old or twenty-nine.

Not Something That Stops Your Progress

You should always be suspicious of someone who is jealous of your time. A demand from a companion that any positive activity——job search, study, early bedtime, abstinence from drugs and alcohol——be stopped or delayed should serve as a bright red warning flag.

Not Daydreams and Fantasies

Staring into space and hallucinating about an adventure with a would-be lover is not only a time stealer, but also can become seriously addictive. This activity is not bad, in itself. Everyone indulges in it at times. However, when you are fantasizing, all other mental activity comes to a grinding halt. Depending on how long and how deeply you have sunk into a particular fantasy, it will take some time to restart the mental engine and get back on course. You can't afford that waste. That time is gone forever.

Not Jealousy

Jealousy shows lack of trust and low self-esteem. One-sided "love" is unhealthy. Try to establish for yourself a new definition for love that includes the condition that it must be a two-way street to qualify as love.

Not a Chance to Escape

For centuries an unhappy home life has been the traditional excuse for "running away to get married." In this age, the rules and the idiom have changed, but the justification remains the same. "If I could just bug out of this hell hole with the screaming kids and the nagging and the filth and the crazy neighbors, everything would be all right. My lover and I could take care of each other and everything would be peaceful and serene." Of course, you know the sequel. You get your own screaming kids, your own nagging partner, your own filth, your own crazy neighbors, and your own empty pocketbook.

The hard road you are now taking is the best road out of poverty. Shortcuts are dangerous and usually have tragic endings.

Not Reform

Love will not reform a partner who is a loser. What you see now is what you get. During the flirtation and courtship period, couples see the best side of each other they will ever see again. They also see a artificiality that will disappear like an ice cube on a hot stove after the chase is over.

A lover strung out on dope or alcohol will hang around your neck like a concrete block; you both will surely sink together. Frequently these sad liaisons begin as self-serving affairs that give the straight partner a feeling of power over the weaker one. Al-Anon is populated with spouses of alcoholics, many of whom subconsciously prolonged their partners' addictions, needing that feeling of being in charge, until the disease finally consumed them both.

Butterflies don't make love to caterpillars. Metamorphosis is the name of the game. (Look it up; in your case it means growth and change.) The whole purpose of this trip is change. As you grow, your standards and tastes in a mate will change drastically. Is it fair for you to make a commitment to someone when you know you will surely have to leave them at the next station? Is your partner mature enough to realize that this may not be the time for marriage, living together, having babies, incurring each other's bills?

HANDLING REJECTION

I believe I've lost more promising counselees through brush-off depression than any other single cause. They felt hemmed in by the hard work their changes required. Their goals began looking impossible. Their standards had gotten higher, but they looked around and saw the same old surroundings. And on top of it all, they began to notice that they were drifting away from old friends. Before, they didn't mind being down in the dumps. Hell, they were part of the dumps. But later, after they'd made so many improvements in their lives, things should have been all better, right?

Active alcoholics, addicts, prisoners, and slum dwellers are all used to rejection and are also used to blaming it on their condition. Many recovered alcoholics have told me that the first great crisis they encountered in their sobriety was rejection. When they were drinking, they could handle being put down by friends or lovers, being refused employment, or being fired. But now they were sober. Now things were supposed to be different.

Rejection is something that will undoubtedly happen, and since it can be predicted, start getting prepared for it now. It is best to think about this during the early "pink cloud" phase of your trip, before the hard work starts and the rough road is exposed. Then you can refer to this little discussion when the time comes. And believe me, it will come! It may be signaled by a creeping deterioration of interest in the goals that you have set, or by increased tardiness or the missing of appointments. Or, one day you may just quit.

Well, what do you do? Members of Alcoholics Anonymous use the *Serenity Prayer* to work through these dangerous dumps. "God, grant me the Serenity to accept the things I cannot change; the courage to change the things I can; and the Wisdom to know the difference." As you repeat that beautiful statement, think on these things:

- Just as all other terrible things that have happened to you in the past are now just memories, this, too, will pass.
- After all you've been through, just what can anyone really do to hurt you?
- How will you feel about this problem a year from now?
- Your growth should be measured from your attitude *before* you started on this trip. Back when you had no plans, no hope.
- Keep shooting at short-term goals, but you must keep your eye on the prize.
- A year from now you'll be a year older whether you turn your life around or not.

WHO IS COUNSELING YOU?

How many teachers and advisors are you listening to? Substance abuse and vocational counselors learn the hard way that when a client leaves their offices that is not necessarily the last counseling session that person will have that day. How many other people are sticking their brush in your bucket?

Ask yourself about your current sources of opinion and advice. It may be family members, friends and acquaintances, spiritual advisors, or it may be a book. Be careful here. People who are not avid readers often will struggle through a single book, then quote it for years.

Do all of your advisors have your best interests at heart? I once spoke with a mother of four who was destitute, although her ex-husband had remarried and was living graciously in their old homestead. She explained that he had convinced her they could save much money if both used *his* attorney for the divorce.

Are you listening to advice from losers or someone on a losing course? Free advice is usually worth what you pay for it. Advisors who have no stock in your growth may give casual counsel that is wrong and may be dangerous. Barroom experts are notorious for giving authoritative tutelage on car repair, world economy, medical problems, legal matters, and job search.

Back in my home town, a county nurse called on a backwoods family to give them much needed advice on sanitation and child care. The mother later told my father how put out she had been at the effrontery of that city-girl nurse. "Imagine her tellin' me how to raise young'uns. Me, who's a'ready *buried five!*"

Always be wary of counsel that begins with "They say . . . " Who are "they?"

Change and Privacy

It is important to remember that a change in the direction of your life and career goals is a very private matter! When someone gives you advice that you know or suspect is wrong, don't argue. You are not out to become the Lone Ranger in charge of turning everyone's life around.

If you decide you are not going to take a particular piece of advice or suggestion from a counselor you do like and trust, make sure you are comfortable in telling him or her of that decision. Much precious time can be wasted on both sides if your counselor mistakenly believes your are following a plan of action she has suggested or approved.

14

MOVING ON

The purpose of this book is to get you into a job that is on your career path. But that's not the whole purpose. A career path, like recovery from alcohol or drugs, is a continuing process that you will pursue throughout your life. The search for sobriety does not end when one decides to quit drinking. Neither does occupational recovery stop with getting your first good job.

Alcoholics who have been sober for ten years probably will not spend as much time on their recovery or concentrate their attention on abstinence as totally as those in their first year. Nevertheless, holders of ten-year chips have cultivated built-in alarm systems that signal when danger is present, or when they should attend a meeting or talk with their sponsor.

So it is with the newly-sober job seeker or vocational virgin. Unless you are a nun or monk with a vow of perpetual poverty and silence, you probably will have several job changes in your life. And unless you die with your boots on, you will eventually be faced with retirement, which is a whopper of a career change.

Once you get a job, you will work at it one day at a time and give it your best shot. But you also will have filed away the very real probability that you will be looking for work again in months, years, or decades. More on that later. First things first!

In the job search techniques explained in Part I, there are some steps that follow in logical order. However, you probably will find yourself using the "cafeteria" method most of the time. This entails absorbing all of this text's suggested strategies and methods, tailoring them to your present capabilities and needs, and then feeding on them as occasion, opportunity, and necessity demand or permit.

I realize that many of you do not consider yourselves recovered substance abusers and that Part I of this book is primarily addressed to sober alcoholics. Do yourself a favor and study it anyway. From an employer's point of view, the reluctance to hire a recovered alcoholic or a vocational virgin stems from the same roots. Prejudice has little to do with it; unpleasant experiences have a lot to do with it. Do not confuse the two terms.

Unless the employer is very new to the game, experience has taught him or her an expensive lesson on odds. The odds are that if the employer hires men or women who have been drunks or drug users, the recruits will quit or have to be terminated before their production repays their training costs. Similarly, the odds are that people who have never held a steady job or have only worked sporadically since leaving school also will quit or have to be terminated before their production repays their training costs.

If an employer is given this kind of derogatory information about an applicant, and has little else to go on, and has the choice of hiring someone else, he or she will always select someone with proven reliability—Mr. or Ms. Clean.

INCREASING YOUR ODDS

Most rejected job applicants are shot down on derogatory information they voluntarily and unnecessarily provide the employer! You can get hired in spite of those odds if you follow four simple rules.

1. Limit the bad or unflattering information available to the employer.

2. Increase the positive or good information available to the employer.
3. Sweeten the pot by agreeing to start at a modest wage.
4. Eliminate all negative elements of the interview that are under your control: (a) hygiene factors discussed in chapters 1 and 11; (b) bizarre clothes, hair style, and jewelry; (c) tardiness; and (d) ignorance of the company, its products and function.

TRAINING PROGRAMS

All aspects of occupational training discussed in chapter 3 apply to the vocational virgin. Many of you probably will qualify for training programs geared to the disadvantaged. But be extremely careful that you are not registering for one of these programs *just* because you are eligible. It is an unfortunate reality that training programs are frequently created as the result of availability of money and training resources, rather than in response to an employment need in the community. We have watched helplessly while men and women struggled through totally impractical classes in jewelry assembly, assertiveness development, and building services.

We've got a small emergency down here. We have three open slots in the 'Poodle Grooming School' starting this afternoon. Do you have anyone qualified as 'disadvantaged' in your waiting room? My friends, I really received that phone call!

JOB EXPERIENCE

Job experience, of course, was what those people in my waiting room really needed. We have heard politicians put down fast-food franchises as "dead end" jobs. They proclaim tearfully that those chain restaurants treat their employees like slaves; starving them by paying the minimum wage.

In the first place, fast-food outlets usually pay considerably above the minimum wage. Secondly, they are blue-chip corporations that spend millions on training. And finally, but foremost from your point of interest, *they hire and train vocational virgins.* If you were an employer trying to fill an entry level position, which of the following documents would impress you most?

This:

CERTIFICATE OF ATTENDANCE

COUNTY VOCATIONAL
PHONOGRAPH ASSEMBLY

Or, this?

To Whom It May Concern:

This will introduce Wendy B. Burger, who has been in our employ for nine months. Wendy is a good worker, a fast learner, and is well liked by co-workers and customers.

She is always at work on time, and on the rare occasions she has had to take unscheduled leave, she has called in early so we could to make adjustments on her shift. She volunteers for jobs outside her normal duties and has expressed an interest in learning more about the fast-food business.

"We have been considering Wendy for management training, and would be sorry to see her leave our operation. I am sure she would be a great asset to any company fortunate enough to hire her."

Sincerely,
Ronald McPizza, Manager

It would be wonderful to retire in thirty years as a vice president of McDonald's or to pass a successful Pizza Hut franchise on to a daughter and her husband after retirement. But in reality, this reference is what Wendy B. Burger was shooting for. This letter, or one like it, is the key to the outside world. Similar entry level jobs may be available at supermarkets, variety stores, and large service stations. The reason for working is working.

The belief that you can't raise a family and have a home in the suburbs on a K-Mart clerk's salary is probably true. Neither can you raise a family and afford a home in the suburbs while going to Harvard Law School. **It's that piece of paper that counts.** The good reference letter from a reputable company is your sheepskin diploma.

EVERY JOB IS A TRAINING EXPERIENCE

Every job must be treated as a training adventure. Everything you do should be filtered through the question, "How is this going to affect that beautiful piece of paper?"

Come to Work

You must come to work. Childish advice, you say? Ninety-five percent of the vocational virgins who are fired from entry-level jobs or screw up any chance of a good reference get that way by just not showing up! You must come to work every day, never taking off because you are tired, bored, or because someone proposed an alternative day's entertainment.

Mentally walk yourself through the three things that will happen at your place of business if you fail to show up:

1. The hasty calls for a replacement—calls to some reliable employee who will now get overtime and a marvelous reference when he or she looks for a better job
2. The boss having to fill in at the counter or production line, neglecting his managerial paperwork, and getting very upset

3. Earning a reputation for unreliability that will take many months of fault-free work and good attendance to erase

On the rare occasion when you must take off work due to illness or extreme emergency, you will always call in, and well ahead of your normal starting time. You will talk directly to the boss; no chicken-hearted, ". . . tell the boss I'm not coming in. My Aunt Bessie's got the blue goofus and I got to take care of her." You will *never* have someone else call in for you! Employers are always suspect and peeved when a third party calls someone in sick.

Be at Work on Time

There is rarely a good excuse for being late; there is never a good excuse for being late twice! And here is an important point: *You will make it a habit to show up when others have an excuse for taking off, such as a heavy snow storm, or a hurricane watch.* That kind of special reliability is really noticed by a boss, and will be etched in his memory at reference writing time.

Be Ready to Work

You will always be ready to work at the beginning of your shift. We have seen men break their necks to get to work on time, then, once inside the door, they will take a coffee break. We've also known women who came through the door exactly at starting time, looking like they just rolled out of bed——no make-up and hair in curlers. The first stop——at least a twenty-minute one——was the ladies' room to complete a tardy preparation for the day.

Talk Shop

While at work, you will talk "shop." No bitching about working conditions or pay. Let the politicians worry about the minimum wage. You will refrain from personal conversations in front of the boss or customers, and you will never engage in an argument within earshot of a customer. If a disagreement with a co-worker erupts and it is of a nature that might jeopardize your job and that good referral, it must be taken to the boss immediately. Otherwise, it's not worth it. The person you have a beef with is not on the same career track as you are.

Excel at Every Task

No matter what the job, you will make every effort to be the best. This point serves a dual function. The first, of course, is to transit successfully out of vocational virginity.

Equally important is the fact that a worker enjoys doing what he knows he does well. People who dread going to work usually have not learned their job well or feel they cannot do their job well. This is especially true of new employees. Old hands are busy working around them, and they stand there like a bump on a log, feeling foolish and useless.

This feeling usually disappears as certain aspects of the job are learned, but many unnecessarily carry that dread far into their work experience. It is the most common *honest* reason for quitting a job. I can vividly remember the first week on every job I've had. I didn't know how to look busy and I didn't know how to goof off. The boss usually walked me through my job once, then got busy with managerial work, relying on my experienced co-workers to carry on with the training.

Co-workers are rarely teachers. Since they don't teach well, they don't like to teach. Besides, it is so much easier to do it than it is to explain how it is done. Another problem is ego. The co-workers are being asked to share an experience they worked hard to master, and that they now enjoy because they are good at it. A third, less prevalent problem is job security. Some marginal employees are forever paranoid that new people are being brought in to replace them.

Here's how to get around that problem. Single out a co-worker that is both good at the job and friendly. Ask that co-worker questions about every aspect of the job. You will not be concerned that others tease you about your diligence or resent your apparent efforts to outdo them. Your eye is on the prize, that beautiful little piece of paper!

Befriend All Employees

If necessary, you will fantasize that even the most unattractive or dull co-worker may be an important personnel recruiter in disguise. In fact, many employers get much of their input on employee performance from co-workers. It is presumed that you will be on your best behavior when in the boss's presence. He or she will want to know how you're making out when *not* under direct supervision. "How's that new man, E.Z. Duzzit, getting along, Fleener?" If E.Z. has been treating Fleener with respect, asking him polite questions, deferring to his experience, and calling him by name, Fleener's response will always be positive.

Your Work Space

Your work space should reflect pride. This means you will take personal responsibility for keeping it clean and orderly, even if it isn't part of your designated duties. If you use an employees' toilet and it is dirty, you clean it. During a slow period you pick up a broom. You might ask your manager, "Ms. Whipdriver, would it be all right if I washed the windows? They're a mess." To detractors who call you a bootlicker, apple-polisher, or brown-noser, you simply respond that you are spending a third of your day in this workplace, and you're not used to living in a mess.

Ask About Advancement

You will always be knowledgeable of advancement procedures and opportunities, and you will make management aware of your interest. You will privately ask your manager and visiting officials about advancement possibilities. You will ask about opportunities for training. If it appears that there are no chances for advancement—that this really is a dead end job—you will double your efforts at excellence and impressing the boss. This is because you will definitely need that beautiful piece of paper before too long.

Identify jobs former employees have gone to from this place. You may find some examples that match your career path. Some examples: A Wendy's counter person was hired as a waitress by

Shoney's. With that experience she became a waitress at a large Holiday Inn, and is now a hotel management trainee. A stock clerk at K-Mart progressed to sales clerk in the household department. With that experience he qualified as a sales person in a well-known home improvement center with a large building contractor clientele. He is now working for one of his former customers, and aspires to be a contractor.

THE PERPETUAL JOB SEARCH

You will always be looking for work. Your job search will continue in an active or passive mode for the rest of your life. Except for a few farmers, doctors, and priests, very few of us get through life with a single vocation. You will not be a "job hopper," but will quietly, carefully, and very privately conduct a continuous job search while you are building work experience and good, solid references.

You will not broadcast to your boss and co-workers that you are looking for a better job elsewhere. As far as they are concerned, you intend to work there for ever and ever.

You will not quit before you have another job sewn up. We have seen several job search manuals and articles that dispensed the alarming advice that one should not look for work while working. The shaky logic is that it would be unfair to one's current boss to look for work while on his payroll, and that a potential new employer would resent this ungrateful tactic used against a fellow businessperson. What garbage!

Looking for work while working eliminates one enormous question in the minds of all interviewers. "If you're so great, why aren't you working?" Admittedly, it will present some problems regarding interview scheduling, but understanding employers who are anxious to hire the best will usually adjust to fit your timetable. It is much more comfortable looking for work from the vantage point of having a job than in the panic of unemployment.

Treat your job search as a legitimate second job. Give it regular time and attention, and don't use your interim employment as an excuse for postponing your real upward trip.

LEAVE THEM LOVING YOU

The first job is not a rut, it is a rung. You will need that same good reference repeatedly as you move up on your career ladder. If you encounter a particular rough stretch of road on your journey, you may even want that job back temporarily.

15

THE MOMENT OF TRUTH

If your journey up and out of poverty succeeds to the point of your first real job experience, you already will have had serious thoughts about "moving out"——changing your residence. Dissatisfaction with living conditions may have been the primary motivation that brought you to the decision to move up and out.

In those days of little hope and poor information all of your problems and obstacles were blamed on living conditions and your immediate environment. Your paramount objective was to cut that umbilical cord. If you could just get away, everything would start to come together. Will you move out of the frying pan and into the fire? Will the drive to get out of where you live cover up honest examination of what you are getting into?

We once worked with a woman who was so anxious to be free of living with an "extended family" of fourteen drinking, drugging, fighting, futile souls that she took her first paycheck and moved into the first available furnished room. She had moved directly into another rat-infested, drug-ridden, filthy hovel.

Whatever your age, your first permanent job will require some sober, grown-up thinking about money. Many of you may never have considered earning more than you spend in a week or a day. Now you'll think about establishing credit, and paying bills on time to keep that credit. The inability to postpone pleasure is a symptom sociologists have long associated with the permanently poor. Saving for something worthwhile is exciting, but it must be learned. When that first paycheck comes along, you will have to learn to "pay yourself first." That means, to put something away in a savings account, immediately.

Shakespeare's Polonius instructed his son to, "Neither a borrower nor a lender be." You will soon have eloquent pitchmen pleading with you to buy on credit. Will you jump out of the frying pan of poverty into the fire of debt?

Alcoholism, drug, and vocational counselors all know that as the time of formal counselor/client relationship draws to a close, concern is felt for the counselee's future selection of people, places, and things. This is because they have so often watched helplessly as bad choices of friends, hangouts, and events reversed progress and turned hard-won achievements into ashes.

Substance abuse counselors are especially anxious because they know that all of the motivation, determination, and job-search techniques they may have passed on to someone they've worked with will mean nothing if their clients walk out the rehabilitation door and pick up another drink or drug. And, so, we start preparing them for that critical moment of separation from the first session. Success has much competition.

DEFYING THE NATURAL STATE

I heard a lecture by an astronomer one time in which he described the slowing down of the universe——the attempt of all matter to return to its natural state of quiet motionlessness. Thinking smaller, the only reason a watch works is that it is trying to run down and stop——thus returning to its natural state. If it ever stops trying to release the tension on the mainspring or relieve the pressure of electrons from its batteries, it will quit telling time.

The natural state for the emerging vocational virgin is to be living in poverty, and the natural state for a newly sober alcoholic is to be drunk. The moment you start letting your guard down, you, too, may begin to return to your natural state——then slowly and surely, like the disease that it is, it will recaim your body, your mind, and your soul.

If alcoholics do not keep the sobriety clock wound tightly with constant reminders of who they are and what they are, the disease returns to its natural, active, acute stage following the brief remission they have enjoyed. Similarly, someone who has been raised to accept poverty and the slavery of welfare as a normal and natural lot will slide back into that comfortable prison if the goals are forgotten and the memory of misery fades.

Good Intelligence

You have learned the importance of good intelligence in this battle for survival. You must know more about yourself than anyone else knows or can find out. The sole purpose of good intelligence is to eliminate unpleasant surprises. The pressures to succeed in a job search, both imagined and real, are immense. Gone are the excuses for failure. Even the most reliable and comfortable excuses—being crazy, drunk, poor, or discriminated against—were at least a sanctuary to which you could retreat when faced with rejection. Now even these are gone. Now comes the moment of truth. And you have prepared yourself for every eventuality as thoroughly as if—no, *because*—your life depends upon it.

Cynical counselors have been likened to the cowboy who never named his horse, because he knew he might have to eat him someday. They believe that close involvement with their clients is destructive; both to the counselor and to his or her case load. Nevertheless, those of us who have teamed up with a client to work the miracle of metamorphosis have become quite involved. We'll remember these people forever.

Unlike the dilettante counselors for whom counseling is merely a charitable hobby, counselors at all tax-supported rehabs and drop-in centers are paid to give equal service to all clients. High school coaches and music teachers have the same commission. But now and then a boy or girl comes along who is willing to come to the gym early and stay late, or one who asks to use the school piano on weekends for additional practice. There will be one who actually listens to instructions and who dreams of the Olympics or Carnegie Hall.

Coaches and music teachers are always alert for a signal that a student may possess that special seed of determination and character. Coaches and music teachers have always practiced the art of subtle triage. They go about their business of availing resources, equipment, and instruction to all with equanimity, while quietly extending special attention, encouragement, and time to polish the few rough diamonds entrusted to their care.

Triage will occur only in the secret parts of the counselor's mind. There will be no cruel, overt fast and slow tracks to brand the less promising candidates. Yes, we care and we do get involved.

Counselors have failures. Heartbreaking failures. They are conned by slick opportunists who have gone through more counselors than the counselor has had clients. Sometimes they find they have simply made a mistake in evaluating a client. They may be convinced at first that all the ingredients are in place—the hunger, the drive, the ability to sacrifice for a better tomorrow—only to discover down the road that their aspirant is a very persuasive "tavern talker."

After a good and honest effort has been made, and only then, the wise ones do not fear admitting a triage error. They do not hang on to a mistake just to prove a point or to justify time already spent. They may have to reassign a patient to the third tent. This happens. The lines of wounded are long and the time is short. If this decision is reluctantly made, there will be no outward indication that there has been a change in the client's status and his transition back to the third tent will go unnoticed by either client and colleagues.

So it is with you. Only in your case it is you, not a counselor, who has determined that you have the hunger, drive, and stamina that Naomi showed in her climb up and over the wall of poverty.

NAOMI'S SUCCESS

It would be dramatic to conclude this part of the book with a story of how Naomi kept climbing up the ladder of success and is now a rich Wall Street broker. However, that would be untrue.

Now, Naomi is living below the government's arbitrary economic chalk line and is officially designated as "poor." But Naomi has a clean apartment in a safe part of town. Naomi has a car——it's not new, but it's paid for. Naomi has a job; not as a stock broker, but as a nursing assistant in a hospital. Naomi is not a college graduate, but she is taking courses in nursing at the Community College. Naomi has a boyfriend, but no live-in relationship. She told us she didn't need the excess baggage of a man right now, unless he was willing to accept the full and equal responsibilities of husband and father. Naomi may be poor, but she has left her past of poverty behind.

Alcoholics Anonymous says that even if an alcoholic returns to the bottle, a taste of their program will screw up his drinking. He will never be able to enjoy that pastime again.

If you are just beginning your trip up and out of poverty and into the world of work and responsibility, be forewarned. The experience of personal salvage through earnest, diligent, humble, and honest work will forever screw up your ability to be comfortable in poverty. However long you last, wherever you go when you leave your success path, whatever you do with the rest of your life, you will never again be happy as nothing more than just another damn number in the Department of Labor's report on "hard core poverty."

Are you ready?